World Class

'Here is the history that makes our game as unique, as exciting and as colourful as the beautiful islands we call home.'

Scottish Football Museum

JAMES FERGUSON

World Class

An illustrated history of Caribbean football

Foreword by **Shaka Hislop**

Macmillan Education
Between Towns Road, Oxford, OX4 3PP
A division of Macmillan Publishers Limited
Companies and representatives throughout the world

www.macmillan-caribbean.com
ISBN 13: 978-1-4050-9825-0
ISBN 10: 1-4050-9825-2

Designed and typeset by Baseline Arts Ltd, Oxford

Printed and bound in Thailand

2010 2009 2008 2007 2006
10 9 8 7 6 5 4 3 2 1

Contents

Foreword by Shaka Hislop

When you think of the Caribbean you think of blue skies, golden beaches, bright beautifully coloured houses, cricket, happy smiling people, cold beer, delicious food, sharing a rum and cola with the local fishermen over their recent catch, a refreshingly lazy pace of life. You somehow never think about football.

Football is widely regarded, by people outside of the Caribbean, as our "second sport". Maybe understandably so. Cricket is how we sell ourselves as a region. Cricket unifies the islands like nothing else does. And then there's football.

Thanks to our weather, sport-minded West Indians can play both. We even split our year into cricket season and football season. I played youth cricket, as well as football, with the national under-14 team with Brian Lara (he honed his magnificent shot-making on my bowling!) before we went our separate sporting ways. West Indians play both cricket and football anywhere. We play in parks, on the beaches, in the streets. Anywhere. I have memories of my grandmother telling me off as I limped home with another bloodied toe, my mother waiting patiently with the antiseptic and plasters, my father chuckling in the background. This is a scene that I'm sure has been played out countless times, not only in my house, but throughout the Caribbean. There's football in our blood. Well, what's left of it anyway. These scenarios and many others like it are documented in this book as it tells how we West Indians feel about our football. It will give you an insight into the Caribbean's long love affair with the sport through words and images. Here is the history that makes our game as unique, as exciting and as colourful as the beautiful islands we call home.

I grew up playing football because my friends did. We'd race home from school and play for about an hour or so before the "big fellas" got home from work. We'd then sit there almost in admiration until the street lights came on. Then it was home to do our homework. I went on to represent my high school teams through under-14, under-16 and eventually the 1st XI. At school I'd regularly play in front of crowds of 3,000. At the time there was no pro-league in Trinidad & Tobago, so I gratefully accepted an offer of a soccer scholarship to Howard University in Washington DC. I eventually made my way to England and Reading FC in 1992. A move to Newcastle United followed in 1995. West Ham beckoned in 1998, before I left for Portsmouth in 2002. I'm now enjoying my second spell with the Hammers. My career has seen me as a professional here in the UK for the last 14 years. It has witnessed promotions, championships, player-of-the-year awards, and far too many near misses.

And yet it is only now I can boast of my proudest moment through it all. After finishing fourth in the CONCACAF qualifying group, we were to play Bahrain, the fifth placed Asian qualifier, in a play-off. The prize a place in the World Cup in Germany 2006. A nervy 1-1 in Port-of-Spain on 8 November was quickly followed by a celebration-inspiring 1-0 in Manama on the 12th. A result sparking celebrations never seen before in T&T. And this is a country that has the second largest carnival in the world! We can now boast of being the smallest country ever to grace the World Cup stage, the second country from the English-speaking Caribbean, after Jamaica in 1998, and the fourth Caribbean country in general with Cuba qualifying in 1938 and Haiti in 1974—beating Trinidad & Tobago for that berth after 5 T&T goals were controversially disallowed in Port-au-Prince (I had to put that in, I'm a Trini after all!).

But what does all of this mean to the people of Trinidad and Tobago? It means the world gets to see who we are.

There is little I don't remember from that wondrous night in Manama. The elation of Dennis Lawrence's 49th-minute header, my heart dropping as Russell Latapy's 79th-minute strike cannoned off the cross bar, the nerves pounding as the minutes and seconds counted down. And then the joy of hearing the final whistle. My emotions then got the better of me. Here I was, the little boy who was happiest playing football barefooted in the streets of Diamond Vale, part of my country's most historic sporting achievement. Dwight Yorke and Russell Latapy, my boyhood friends, who also played in that under-14 team with Brian Lara, brought me to tears. I was doing alright until I got to them!

Then came the draw for the group stages of the World Cup.

It had to be fate. The T&T team boasted some 12 players plying their trade in the UK. I was born here and had been playing here for nearly 14 years, Dwight Yorke and his beaming grin will forever be remembered in English football, Chris Birchall was English, his mother being born in Trinidad to English parents. The seeded team in our group—England. I couldn't stop laughing. Then my phone began ringing. It was just about everyone in the team. We were all laughing. On 15 June we'd be lining up against Rooney, Beckham, Gerrard and the rest of the boys most of us could only see on *Match of the Day*. Just when we thought our summer couldn't get any better, it did.

But what does all of this mean to the people of Trinidad and Tobago? It means the world gets to see who we are. The results seem almost secondary. We aren't the Reggae Boyz, we're the Soca Warriors. You see that's the thing with football in the Caribbean, it's how we distinguish ourselves. This is our own identity, our own individuality. As much as we love our cricket, as much as the Windies brings the region together, football can be everything to us. It's how we identify ourselves. And that is the reason football will never be our "second sport". Long after the Reggae Boyz, long after the celebrations in Germany are over and forgotten, West Indians will go to watch our beloved cricket team play, then cross the street for a kick about. Antiseptic and plasters to the ready.

Preface

Caribbean football? When Trinidad & Tobago qualified for the 2006 World Cup finals in Germany, many commentators seemed almost surprised that the Trinidadians played football. Brian Lara, yes–but football? Well, they were wrong. Football is ingrained in the popular culture of Trinidad & Tobago, as it is in Jamaica, Haiti and many other Caribbean territories. Of course, people love cricket, or baseball and basketball, but football is in the mainstream.

Two figures perhaps illustrate the hold that football has in the Caribbean. When researching this book, I was interested to come across an article by the Trinidadian writer Michael Anthony on Eric Williams, the great intellectual and politician who led Trinidad & Tobago to independence in 1962. Williams always had the rather distant image of a man immersed in big ideas and big decisions. But Anthony's piece recalls another Williams, the schoolboy at Queen's Royal College:

> *Not only did he play football for his college but he was captain of the team. He had an outstanding career in the forward line, and the only complaint his team mates had against him was that he always wanted to score.*

When he was taking his all-important scholarship exams, Williams' father was worried that he would be injured if he played football and forbade him to play one afternoon. The young Williams watched from the sidelines, but as a childhood friend recalled, "Our team was losing and Eric said he couldn't stand it. He went home and got his clothes. He played so great that we scored the winning goal."

At the other end of the Caribbean archipelago, another great historical personality was an avid football player and fan. Bob Marley famously claimed that "football is freedom" and played almost every day until his untimely death. Like many Jamaicans of his generation, he was inspired by the creative and free-flowing game played in Brazil and loved the cult of individual brilliance surrounding Pele or Garrincha. His daily routine involved not only informal kickabouts but strict fitness training.

Football is played throughout the region, by schoolchildren, youth teams, parish and village teams, and now professional clubs. Every community has its open space where players congregate once the humidity and heat of the tropical day has subsided. The bigger towns and

Right: "Football is freedom..." Bob Marley on the ball.

cities have stadiums, sometimes rudimentary by European or North American standards, but arenas of passion and drama. Thousands of enthusiasts organize clubs for children of all ages, for women players, for anyone who wants to take part.

From the Caribbean have emerged not just world-class national sides, but a legion of top players who have brought their skills onto the world stage. Many household football names in the UK, Europe and USA are Caribbean-born: from Jamaica and Trinidad & Tobago, from Martinique and Guadeloupe, from Suriname and French Guiana. These footballers have profoundly affected the way in which we watch and appreciate the sport and have enriched it to an extraordinary degree. Without Dwight Yorke or John Barnes, Edgar Davids or Cyrille Regis, the game in Britain would have been much the poorer.

This book aims, through words and pictures, to document and celebrate the Caribbean contribution to world football and to underline that football is as Caribbean as reggae, rum or even cricket.

A NOTE ON GEOGRAPHY

By Caribbean, I mean not only the islands of the archipelago that run down from the Bahamas to Trinidad & Tobago, but also the former colonial enclaves on the mainland of South America—Guyana, French Guiana and Suriname—which are part of Caribbean political organizations and generally have more in common with the islands than the rest of South America. I also include Bermuda, which, though not strictly speaking Caribbean, has many historic connections with the region, is a part of CONCACAF and competes with Caribbean teams. I have not included Belize, as it plays its international football in a Central American grouping.

ACKNOWLEDGEMENTS

I would like to record my thanks to the following who have helped me with their time and views: Clyde Best, Chris Birchall, Russell Latapy, Dennis Lawrence, Stern John and particularly Shaka Hislop. The history of football in Trinidad & Tobago by Valentino Singh on the Trinidad & Tobago Football Federation's website proved a mine of detailed information. The following have been extremely helpful in locating and supplying images: Tinnie Percival (St. Kitts), Shaun Fuentes and Anu Lakhan (Trinidad & Tobago), Chris Bryan (Turks & Caicos Islands), Sterling Swan and David Sabir (Bermuda), Ovid Holder and Frederick Granger (Guyana), Sheree Roden, Bryan Cummings and Ashley Gambrill (Jamaica), Petal Nathaniel (St. Lucia). Louisa Browne at Macmillan Caribbean has worked tirelessly on this project. I am grateful, too, to my son Patrick, already a connoisseur of football and a true fan.

12

Part One

Highs And Lows: The World Stage

Wednesday 16 November 2005

Port of Spain goes wild. Shortly after 2pm local time, the result is confirmed: Bahrain 0 Trinidad & Tobago 1. A single goal from giant defender Dennis Lawrence has settled the two-leg play-off match. The Soca Warriors have qualified for the World Cup finals in Germany in June 2006. This is the smallest country ever to qualify for the World Cup. People spill out onto the streets. Cars are hooting, national flags are waving, school kids and office workers mingle in downtown Port of Spain. The celebrations will go on long into the night. Local writer Nicholas Laughlin notes in his blog:

> *Cars went past with their horns blaring, headlights on in broad daylight, flags streaming from windows. People stood on the side of the road waving flags at passing cars, matador style. Little knots of people had formed outside bars or rumshops. And everywhere: smiles. A friend on the phone from St. James, astonished: "All I can think is, this must be what it was like when the war ended."*

Top to bottom: Soca Warriors celebrate Lawrence's winning goal; the sweet taste of victory; Stern John flies the flag in Manama.

Not quite the end of war, but another sort of victory. When Lawrence rose above the diminutive Bahraini defenders to glance Dwight Yorke's flighted corner kick into the net, it was enough. The game went on for another half hour, increasingly bad-tempered as the Bahrainis had a player dismissed and a late goal disallowed, but the single goal was enough. The stadium at Manama was a cauldron; at the final whistle the Trinidadian team needed police protection as seats were ripped up and thrown onto the pitch. Even the

Right: Drumming up a frenzy on the terraces.

Below: High hopes in the packed Hasely Crawford stadium.

outright hostility shown by the Bahraini fans could not prevent a jubilant Stern John from brandishing the national flag.

Back in Port of Spain the House of Representatives had adjourned so that the honourable members could watch the final half-hour of the match on television in the tea-room. The *Trinidad Guardian* described how Prime Minister Patrick Manning, opposition leader Basdeo Panday and other MPs sat transfixed in front of the screen.

Manning advises our goalie Kelvin Jack as he collects the ball, having thwarted Bahrain's goal-scoring intentions: "Slow it down..."

Arouca South MP Camille Robinson-Regis has been calm so far, but the tension is getting to her.

"We can't afford to relax now," she declares.

She jumps to her feet, just like several other nervous MPs and a chorus of "Ohs!" goes up as a desperate attempt on the T&T goal by Bahrain flies out of touch, off the crossbar...

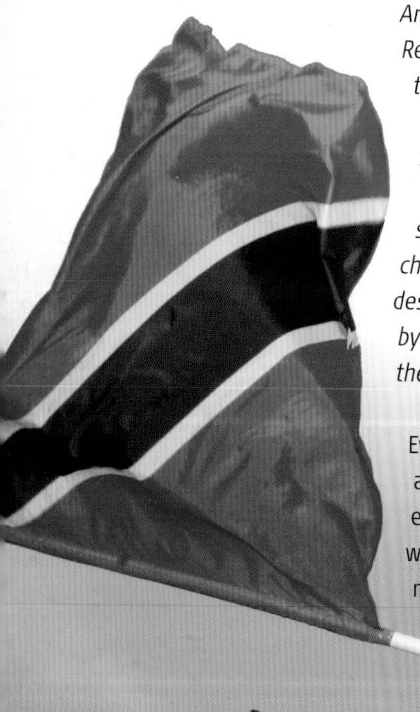

Everyone in Trinidad & Tobago, and many elsewhere, counted every moment until the final whistle. Only then did the magnitude of the achievement sink in. Within hours a relieved PM Manning had announced that Thursday would be a public holiday. He called on people to give the returning players a heroes' welcome, and asked that schoolchildren be allowed to line the road from Piarco Airport into town.

The reception was amazing. The team was greeted by the PM on the tarmac of the airport, where a huge crowd had gathered. Masses of people lined the airport road, waving their red and black flags, cheering and whistling. Soca and steelband music filled the air. Grown men wept. Finally, after a long and sometimes chaotic procession, the motorcade made it to Brian Lara Promenade in downtown Port of Spain where speeches were made and the partying began. Prime Minister Manning spoke a profound truth when he said: "Team Trinidad has done for Trinidad and Tobago what many politicians have failed to do. Bringing together people of every race, class, and persuasion."

Only five days before, it had all seemed so different. Trinidad & Tobago were at home in the first leg against unfancied Bahrain, who had come third in their Asian qualifying group and then beaten Uzbekistan to jump the hurdle into the play-off match. They were footballing unknowns from a small country with no real sporting track record. In the packed Hasely Crawford Stadium surely the physically powerful Trinidadians would overawe and demolish their opponents.

Surely the physically powerful Trinidadians would overawe and demolish their opponents.

Left: Russell Latapy on the ball.

Above: Dwight Yorke feels the heat.

Left: The Trinidad & Tobago team before the home leg.

It was not to be. With veteran Russell Latapy running the midfield, Trinidad & Tobago played a probing game, having the best of the possession and rarely under pressure. But the Bahrainis soaked up their own pressure, defending methodically and frustrating close-range efforts from Dwight Yorke and Stern John. Then after half-time Bahrain did what they do well. A sudden counter-attack ended with a powerful header from Salman Husein. The home crowd was stunned.

Cometh the hour... Six minutes later, the slight figure of Christopher Birchall, born in the English county of Staffordshire and playing for unglamorous Port Vale, got hold of the ball and unleashed a ferocious half-volley from 30 yards into the top left hand corner. 1-1. The crowd re-found its voice, but it was too late. The return game looked daunting. Captain Dwight Yorke sounded resolute, and in hindsight prophetic, when he said "To the people of the Caribbean, this game is far from over. We know we need to score one away goal and our players are capable of doing that."

The first steps on the long road to Germany had been taken in the summer of 2004. Victories against the lightweight Dominican Republic, St. Vincent and St. Kitts & Nevis were to be expected, but then the team lost twice to Mexico, the regional footballing superpower. Then in February and March of 2005 things went badly wrong. First a home defeat to the USA, then an away 5-1 mauling at the hands of Guatemala, and then a goalless draw at home to Costa Rica. Trinidad & Tobago sat bottom of the six-team CONCACAF qualifying group. The World Cup finals seemed little more than a mirage.

"To the people of the Caribbean, this game is far from over. We know we need to score one away goal..."

Above: Alaa Hubail tussles with Carlos Edwards.

Right: Chris Birchall celebrates his long-range equaliser.

From
19

It was time for a shake-up. On 31 March a press release from the Trinidad & Tobago Football Federation announced that coach Bertille St. Clair had been sacked, to be replaced immediately by Dutchman Leo Beenhakker. St. Clair had had 35 matches in charge since his return to the job the previous year, winning 19, losing 13 and drawing 6. But the dismal run of form in the World Cup qualifiers was his undoing. The TTFF, joined by "special advisor" Jack Warner, Trinidad & Tobago's CONCACAF President and FIFA Vice-President, also fired several other personnel, bringing in Latapy as assistant coach. "We have hired the coach to take us to Germany. That is the expectation," announced the TTFF.

Above: Leo Beenhakker offers some touchline advice.

Left: Marvin Andrews in action against Panama in the 2–0 victory, June 2005.

Sixty-three-year-old Beenhakker was a coach with serious pedigree. He had trained and managed Ajax and Feyenoord as well as Real Zaragoza and Real Madrid in Spain. He had won six national titles and had worked with the Dutch national side as well as Saudi Arabia in the 1990s. Even so, the expectations at first looked unlikely to be fulfilled. A victory against Panama was followed by a 2-0 defeat away to Mexico in June and a 1-0 loss in the USA in August. Qualifying looked no more likely than it had in April

But then the team's prospects began to brighten. After stern and stirring words to the players following the defeat by the USA, Beenhakker engineered a 3-2 victory over Guatemala, only to lose 2-0 to Costa Rica. An away 1-0 win in Panama suddenly changed things again in Trinidad & Tobago's favour. The coveted fourth spot in the CONCACAF group seemed in sight if victory could be achieved in the final game. The only problem was that the opposition was—Mexico. To make matters worse, Trinidad & Tobago had to win to be sure of going through, as Guatemala was close behind and was expected to beat Costa Rica at home.

Everyone older than about thirty-five was by now suffering from a nasty case of *déja vu*. Twice before, the national team had been on the verge of qualifying for the World Cup. In 1973, the team, featuring the scoring midfielder Everald "Gally" Cummings, had steamrollered its way through early qualifying games before making it to the second qualifying competition in Haiti in December. There, amidst some of the worst refereeing ever seen (the Salvadorean referee and Canadian linesman were subsequently banned for life), five Trinidadian goals against Haiti were disallowed and numerous penalty claims ignored. The Haitians somehow won 2-1 despite being outclassed. The *Trinidad Guardian* sports reporter ironically remarked "They say goals win matches. This is one time they didn't."

Above: Stern John celebrates his second goal against Mexico.

Right: Dennis Lawrence and Marvin Andrews challenge Mexican goalkeeper Jorge Campos during their 1-0 victory in July 2000.

Everyone older than about thirty-five was by now suffering from a nasty case of déja vu.

To make matters worse, the team then trounced Mexico 4-0, allowing Haiti to progress to the finals in West Germany.

If that was heart-breaking, then the events of November 1989 were nothing short of a national disaster. Costa Rica had already qualified for the Italy 1990 World Cup finals, but a second place was up for grabs, between the USA and Trinidad & Tobago, both on nine points. The Trinidadians, by now coached by Cummings, had been playing well, and a run of victories against Guatemala and El Salvador had boosted hopes. The squad included a young Dwight Yorke, the "Little Magician" Russell Latapy, the brilliant Leroy Spann and captain Clayton Morris, a solid defensive presence. Baptized the "Strike Squad", this was the team to take the twin-island nation to the finals. With Carnival approaching, all the calypso songs were of victory. It just needed a draw in the final game: at home to the Americans.

Nobody who watched or listened on the radio to that game will ever forget. A lucky, harmless-looking long-distance shot from the USA's Paul Caliguiri somehow sailed over goalkeeper Michael Maurice in the 31st minute, and that was it. Trinidad & Tobago could find no way back. As the game ended, players wept openly, but—and here veterans remember this detail with pride—they and the

Below: Dwight Yorke leaves Mexico's Francisco Fonseca behind

crowd congratulated the Americans (a far cry from that torrid night in Bahrain).

Stern John, then a boy, had watched the Strike Force's last-gasp defeat, and like others, the British-based striker would do anything to avert a repeat performance against Mexico. One of many British-based players selected by Beenhakker, Stern had been scoring prolifically throughout the qualifiers. The weight of history was on his and all the other players' shoulders as the critical encounter with Mexico approached. But there were also grounds for some optimism; hadn't Trinidad & Tobago beaten Mexico 1-0 in 2000 in the previous World Cup qualifiers (although they had also lost 7-0)?

On 12 October 2005 the fateful day arrived. The Mexicans, already assured of a place in Germany, fielded a slightly under-strength side, but even so made most of the early running. On 30 minutes Trinidad & Tobago were awarded a penalty, but Stern shot weakly at the goalkeeper. Then, eight minutes later, Jaime Lozano scored with an elegant chip over goalkeeper Kelvin Jack to put the visitors ahead. A dreadful sense of foreboding filled the Hasely Crawford Stadium. But deliverance was at hand—in the form of Stern John, who atoned for his penalty miss just before half time with a tap-in.

The interval brought the news that Guatemala were leading Costa Rica, and this spurred the Trinidadians onto a much more physical and fearless performance than in the first half. After ten minutes the ball was in the back of the Mexican net after Latapy and John combined to penetrate the Mexican defence, but the goal was disallowed. And then, after an hour, John scored again, this time after incisive play by Latapy and with a vicious shot that transfixed the stadium. 2-1 it remained, and Trinidad & Tobago might even have scored a third, when John's opportunistic back heel was cleared off the line. The Soca Warriors had earned the tie with Bahrain.

...he made us believe that we can be a better team...

What had Beenhakker done that St. Clair hadn't? "We are a new T&T since he arrived," said young striker Scott Sealy. "We play a different way now, more disciplined, more organized." Certainly, the veteran Dutchman's ability to change the team around to suit the fixture and to make the telling substitution made a big difference. When in the second leg of the Bahrain game he dropped Latapy in favour of the 20-year-old Kenwyne Jones, he ran the risk of incurring the public's wrath. But the change paid off, as Jones' pace worried the opposition. And when Latapy came on for the last fifteen minutes it proved to be a tactical masterstroke, allowing Trinidad & Tobago to hold much more possession and frustrate the Bahrainis.

Beenhakker was also astute enough to accept Bertille's decision to talk veterans Latapy and Yorke out of international retirement and to add their enormous experience to the youth and energy of other players. The selection of Yorke as captain, in particular, was crucial, as he had as much experience at the top level with Manchester United as any player in the world. In this way Beenhakker built a collective team spirit that was strong enough to rebound from adversity and positive enough to create self-belief.

If before, under St. Clair, there had been problems of consistency and self-discipline, Beenhakker's no-nonsense and methodical

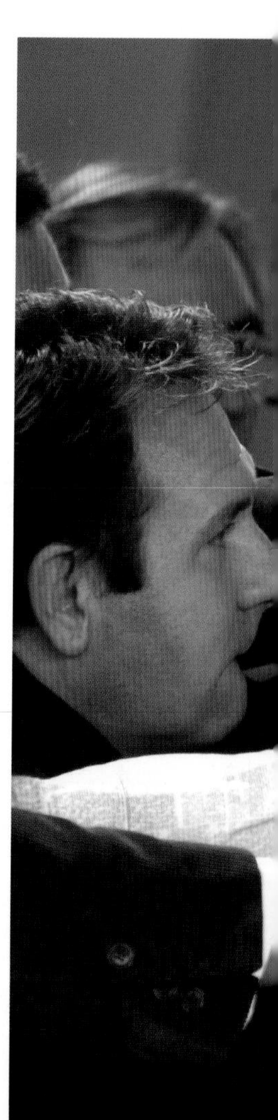

approach curbed excessive individualism and made the team play as a cohesive unit. The Dutchman, famous for his short fuse and impatience with journalists, was not afraid to give his players a tongue-lashing as well as delivering inspirational pep talks. Yorke spoke after the Bahrain game about a mix of Trinidad spirit and Dutch tactics. Beenhakker was no doubt influenced by the Dutch concept of "total football"—the prioritizing of collective teamwork over individual positions—but he was in no sense a cold theoretician. His ability to inspire his players was the crucial factor.

As goalkeeper Kelvin Jack put it:

> *He changed the mind-set of the players and psychologically he made us believe that we can be a better team and all of the players took that on board and were able to produce that on the pitch. Not every game we did well but he brought that fighting spirit, that tactical awareness and that self-belief that we could do this.*

*

Below: Beenhakker faces the press.

Above: Cuban captain Manuel Chorens exchanges pennants with Romania's Gheorghe Rasinaru before the 3-3 draw.

Trinidad & Tobago's moment of glory will long be remembered by players and fans alike. But it is also worth recalling that this achievement is part of a wider story of success on the part of Caribbean football.

The Caribbean first burst onto the world footballing stage in the somewhat unlikely form of... Cuba. Most people, of course, associate the island with baseball rather than football, and it is true that baseball is really the national sport. But in 1938 a bizarre series of events allowed the Cuban national football team to go to the World Cup finals in France.

In that year the threat of world war hung heavily over Europe. Hitler and Mussolini were in bellicose mood, and it seemed only a matter of time before conflict would break out. FIFA decided that the third-ever World Cup finals should be held in France, fearful that any other European country would try to use the event as a propaganda exercise, as Italy had done in 1934. Argentina had applied to stage the finals, but FIFA ruled against the South Americans, who promptly boycotted the event. They were followed by a host of nations, who either did not wish to travel to war-threatened Europe or for one reason or another did not want to participate. (Strangely, England declined to take part, as the national Football Association was not part of FIFA and in any case thought that winning the competition would be a sheer formality.)

Among those teams to cold-shoulder the 1938 finals was the USA, who had got as far as the semi-finals in the 1930 Uruguay competition, but did not want to become involved in a European political minefield. The same worry probably motivated the teams from the regional Group 11, Subgroup B—Colombia, Costa Rica, Mexico, El Salvador and Dutch Guiana (now Suriname)—who all pulled out. Which left Cuba with a walkover and a ticket to France without playing a game.

So it was that the amateur Cubans, managed by José Tapia, lined up against fancied Romania at the Chapou stadium in the southern city of Toulouse on 5 June 1938. It was a free-scoring contest in front of 7,000 spectators, of whom almost none were Cuban. In the end, a goal by Juan Tunas in the 21st minute of extra time brought the game to a 3-3 conclusion. If that was good for the Cubans, better was to follow. In the replay four days later Hector Socorro and Carlos Oliveira scored to achieve a memorable 2-1 victory.

The result was all the more impressive, given that Tapia had inexplicably dropped the player whom most thought was the star of the first game: goalkeeper Benito Carvajales. Not to be outdone, Carvajales summoned journalists to his own personal press conference, where he confidently predicted that Cuba would triumph in the replay: "The Romanian game has no more secrets for us," he claimed, "we shall score twice, they will only score once. *Adios caballeros.*" He was eerily accurate, even if most present thought that the Cuban goal was offside.

If the Cubans thought they were on a lucky run they were wrong. In fact, their luck was out. The quarter-final draw pitted them against Sweden, one of the most consistent sides of the 1930s. Worse, the Swedes had enjoyed a bye in the first round because Austria, recently annexed by Hitler's Germany, had withdrawn at the last moment, leaving only 15 teams in the competition. The Swedes were fresh; the Cubans exhausted after their two-match heroics. The final score was 8-0, with Gustav Wetterström and Tore Keller both scoring hat-tricks. It could even have been worse, as the recalled Carvajales saved a penalty. One French journalist, Georges Capdeville, who witnessed the rout at Antibes' Fort Carré stadium on 12 June memorably remarked "Up to five goals is journalism. After that, it becomes statistics."

While Sweden, coached by the Hungarian-born Josef Nagy, celebrated their statistical landslide, the Cuban team made the long trip home to a muted reception. It was the island's one and only appearance in a World Cup final. Sweden lost 5-1 to Hungary in the semi-finals and then 4-2 to Brazil in the third place play-off game. The tournament was won by Italy.

"The Romanian game has no more secrets for us... we shall score twice, they will only score once.

Since then the Cubans have never managed to qualify again. By regional standards, they are a strong team, but like much else, football has been adversely affected by politics. Fidel Castro's revolution, a forty-plus-year economic embargo and a siege mentality have not helped the sport in an island that in any case is in love with baseball. There is no professional football in Cuba, and few, if any, Cubans have made it overseas. All too often, players tend to use overseas trips as an opportunity to "disappear" and claim political asylum.

*

England was *the* team to beat in the 1950s. After the Second World War the English FA rejoined FIFA and condescended to take part in the 1950 World Cup, to be held in Brazil. The English qualified top of a group completed by Scotland, Wales and Northern Ireland.

Their recent form was good, and the team, including such legends as Sir Stanley Matthews, Billy Wright and Tom Finney, was confident of success. In its group in Brazil England found itself up against Spain, Chile and the USA, who had qualified by beating Mexico and Cuba. The USA, it was fair to say, was hardly considered a footballing giant, and in their first match the Americans went down 3-1 to Spain. England, on the other hand, comfortably dispatched Chile with a score of 2-0.

Next up for England was the USA on 29 June at the south-eastern city of Belo

Above: Alf Ramsey looks on... as (below) Joe Gaetjens' historic goal leaves Bert Williams stranded.

Horizonte. To say that the English were expected to win was an understatement; to say that the result was a surprise was more than an understatement. When the final whistle blew the USA had triumphed by one goal to nil. Such was the disbelief around the world, so it is said, that one London editor, on seeing the result come in on the wire, thought it a mistake and wrote that England had won 10-1. The Brazilian crowd was jubilant at England's disaster and chaired the Americans off the pitch.

...the man who scored the goal was not actually an American.

But the man who scored the goal was not actually an American. He was from the Caribbean—from Haiti, to be precise.

Joseph Edouard Gaetjens was born in Port-au-Prince on 19 March 1924 to a Haitian

Below: The USA team lines up at Belo Horizonte.

Left: Gaetjens is chaired off the pitch.

mother and Belgian father. In 1948 he moved to New York City to study accounting at Columbia University on a Haitian government scholarship, but instead found himself washing dishes in a German restaurant. The restaurant owner heard that Gaetjens liked football and fixed up a trial for a local team, Brookhatten. There his speed and instinct for goal won instant recognition, and he ended up top scorer in the American Soccer League in 1949. From there it was a short step to selection for the national team, an assortment of semi-professionals including a car mechanic and a hearse driver, paid $5 a day for their football skills.

It seems that nobody bothered to check Gaetjens' nationality. In any event, in the 1950s, a would-be US citizen only had to state "intent" to be considered American.

Gaetjens did not get onto the scoresheet in the game against Spain, but on that day in June 1950 he made history. Team mate and midfielder Walter Bahr recalls what happened: "I took a shot. It was going to the far post. The goalkeeper had to move to his right to get the ball and somehow Joe Gaetjens came from that side and deflected it with his head." The diving header wrongfooted Bert Williams and sailed into the goal. Having survived an English onslaught for the first half hour before the goal, the Americans (and one Haitian) weathered a further siege, with England hitting bar or post three times.

Finally, after an eternity for the Americans, the game was over and mighty England had lost, in the words of the *Daily Mail*'s correspondent, to a "team I never knew played football". England went on to lose 1-0 to Spain and returned home, suitably chastened. The USA were soundly beaten, 5-2, by Chile, and Gaetjens failed to find the net. The English media were horrified by what had happened; the result just about made the fourth page in the *New York Times* sport section.

After the World Cup Gaetjens played professional football for Racing Club de Paris and played for Haiti against Mexico in a 1953 qualifying game. He eventually returned to Haiti in 1954, where he opened a dry-cleaning business in the capital Port-au-Prince. The country at that time was in political turmoil and in 1957, backed by the army, "Papa Doc" Duvalier came to power in rigged elections. With the help of his private henchmen, the "Tontons Macoutes", Duvalier established a particularly vicious dictatorship. Gaetjens by all accounts was not interested in politics, but members of his family had worked for an opponent of Duvalier in the 1957 election, and his mother and a brother were arrested soon afterwards, while other family members fled Haiti. Gaetjens decided to stay—to his cost. On 8 July 1964 as he was opening his business, he received a visit from several armed policemen. "When he arrived, they rushed to his car, put a gun on his head, and drove to the Port-au-Prince police station," recalled his brother Jean-Pierre Gaetjens, who escaped to Spain. Joe was never seen again, just one more victim of "Papa Doc's" death squads.

Gaetjens was inducted into the US Soccer Hall of Fame in 1976. In 1979 the Inter-American Commission on Human Rights concluded in a report that "The Fact that Mr. Gaetjens, a football player of international standing, has not been seen since his detention in 1964 leads to conclusion that he is dead."

In the 1950s, a would-be US citizen only had to state "intent" to be considered American.

Ten years after Joe Gaetjens disappeared, football fans were at fever pitch in Haiti. Haitians might have been living in dire poverty and under the repressive regime of "Baby Doc" (son of "Papa Doc") Duvalier, but at least their team had qualified for the 1974 World Cup finals in West Germany.

"Baby Doc", it was rumoured, was bank-rolling the team, paying the group of talented amateurs out of his own, admittedly very full, pocket as they cruised through the CONCACAF qualifying rounds. First they routed Puerto Rico (not really, of course, a footballing island) by 7-0 and 5-0. Then in late 1973, in a series of games, conveniently held in Port-au-Prince, the Haitians overcame the Netherlands Antilles (3-0) and—in a débâcle of a match—Trinidad & Tobago (2-1). Next came the Central Americans: Haiti beat Honduras 1-0 and then Guatemala 2-1. With this sort of form, the Haitians began to believe they could qualify, and when Trinidad & Tobago humiliated mighty Mexico in a classic 4-0 victory, Haiti went mad. It hardly mattered that they themselves lost to Mexico four days later: they had eight points, while Trinidad & Tobago and Mexico had six apiece.

So it was Haiti, along with Australia and Zaire, that made its debut in West Germany's finals. The team was young, gifted and highly motivated. All played for local teams with the exception of captain Wilner Nazaire, who occasionally appeared for French first division side Valenciennes. Goalkeeper Henri Francillon was highly rated, as was midfielder Philippe Vorbe. But the star was Emmanuel "Manno" Sanon, whose goals had fired Haiti into the finals.

Right: The Haitian team lines up for the national anthem.

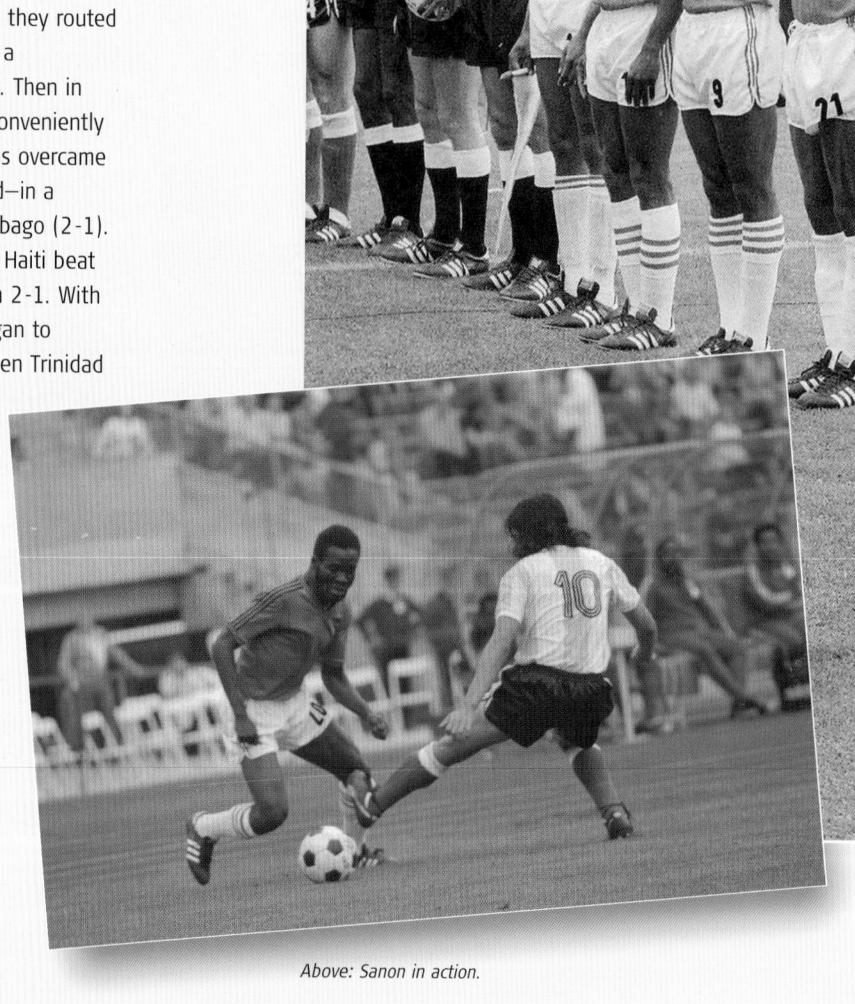

Above: Sanon in action.

It was Haiti, along with Australia and Zaire, that made its debut in West Germany's finals. The team was young, gifted and highly motivated.

Above: Zoff can only watch as Sanon scores for Haiti.

Right: Pietro Anastasi makes it 3-1 to Italy.

Born into a poor Port-au-Prince family in 1951, Sanon played with the Don Bosco club in the posh suburb of Pétionville, where his speed and appetite for goal caught the eye of former Racing Club Haïtien player and national coach, Antoine Tassy.

If the Haitians were euphoric on making the finals, they received a sobering reminder of the task in hand when they learned that they would face Italy, Poland and Argentina in their group. They also received the rather unwelcome news that their request for a bonus of $5,000 per player had been angrily turned down by "Baby Doc", who instead handed out land titles to each footballer at a ceremony at the Sylvio Cator stadium. (Unfortunately, the land turned out to be useless marshland.) The players, the dictator said, would perform their patriotic duty in Germany—or else.

The first game was against mighty Italy, runners-up in 1970. In goal was the legendary Dino Zoff, who had just completed twelve full internationals without conceding a single goal. The daunting fact was that Zoff had played 1,143 minutes of top-level football with a clean sheet. If ever there was a David and Goliath contest it was on 15 June 1974 at the imposing Olympiastadion in Munich in front of over 50,000, largely Italian, fans.

"I beat the defender with my speed. One-on-one with Dino Zoff, and the goal was wide open."

In the first half Haiti survived wave after wave of Italian attacks. At half-time it was 0-0. Then, in the 46th minute, something almost miraculous happened.

As Sanon himself recalled:

With my pace, you can't leave me with just one defender, but that is what happened. I was one-on-one with Spinosi. I received a pass from Philippe Vorbe. I beat the defender with my speed. One-on-one with Dino Zoff, and the goal was wide open. I dummied to go left, and then went right. I rounded him, and rolled the ball into the net.

Italians, watching the game live on TV, were aghast; Haitians, almost all listening on radio, were ecstatic. The least fancied team in the contest was leading one of the favourites. For six heroic minutes Haiti led, then Italy equalized. Then an own-goal gave the Italians the lead, which they solidified in the 79th minute with a goal from substitute Pietro Anastasi of Juventus.

The defeat was an anti-climax, but worse was to come. The next day, defender Jean Joseph tested positive for a banned substance (it was, he claimed, an asthma medication). This enraged an army colonel—presumably a minder sent with the team by "Baby Doc"—who slapped Joseph, provoking a general melee in the team's hotel. With their morale rapidly evaporating and fearful of reprisals back in Haiti, the Haitians lost heavily to Poland (7-0) and, more creditably, to Argentina (4-1), with Sanon scoring the consolation goal.

The Haitian team returned home, with no points gained and a goal deficit of 14-2, but at least Sanon went down in footballing history as "the man who beat Dino Zoff". For six minutes, Haiti had been a world-beating side. Sanon himself went on to play professional football for Germinal Beerschot in Antwerp, Belgium, and in the US before returning to Haiti, where he has since worked as a coach.

As for Haiti, it remains as football-mad as it was in 1974, with most Haitians idolizing the Brazilian national side as well as their own. But the impoverished country, wracked by political turmoil and deprivation, has struggled to mount another successful bid to get to the World Cup. Its league football carries on regardless, even though starved of resources, while courageous individuals such as ex-political prisoner and football fan Bobby Duval have done their best to improve the lives of Haitian children by introducing them to the sport in Port-au-Prince's worst slum areas.

Below: Poland's Jerzy Gorgon dispossesses Sanon during the 7-0 rout.

Below: The Jamaican team.

France, 1998, and at last a team from the English-speaking Caribbean was at the World Cup finals. Jamaica, aka the Reggae Boyz, booked a place in the 32-team competition after a long and gruelling qualification that began with double victories over Suriname and Barbados. The success continued in the next phase in September 1996 with a convincing 3-0 victory in Kingston over Honduras. Five games later, Jamaica was into the final round of the CONCACAF qualifying tournament, with another ten games to play. Victories over Canada, Costa Rica and El Salvador, plus draws against the USA (twice), Canada, El Salvador and Mexico gave the Jamaicans 14 points and third place in the table behind Mexico and the USA. Third was good enough to qualify.

It was a steep learning curve for the players and for the Brazilian technical director, "Professor" Rene Simoes, who began work with the Jamaicans in 1994. He was not the first foreign coach, nor the first Brazilian to take over the Jamaican national side (George

Penna had experienced some success in the mid-1960s). But, in collaboration with national coach Carl Brown, Simoes stamped his authority and personality on the team. Amidst a huge number of qualifying games as well as friendlies the Brazilian insisted that the team play free-flowing, cultured football in the Brazilian mould. He insisted on discipline as well. He also had the courage, despite huge controversy, to drop local favourites Walter Boyd and Onandi Lowe and to bring in four foreign-based players of Jamaican descent:

"The team should play free-flowing, cultured football in the Brazilian mould."

Robbie Earle, Deon Burton, Paul Hall and Fitzroy Simpson. The gamble paid off, as Derby County's Burton scored in the crucial wins against Costa Rica and Canada and draws with the USA and El Salvador.

Simoes' own brand of charisma and guile, together with the forceful personality of Captain Horace Burrell, had gradually created the impetus that brought the Reggae Boyz to the finals. Their nickname (allegedly coined by a Zambian journalist while the team was playing a friendly there) pointed to the strongly patriotic feeling that ran through team and fans alike. And as Jamaica, all too often divided rather than united, began to get behind the team, so too did government and private-sector sponsors, hoping to benefit from the feel-good factor that football glory might being.

Below: The Ouch Girls add their support.

gyrating Ouch Girls), and won a great many friends.

Robbie Earle's account of the run-up to the games offers an intriguing insight into the clash of personalities between coach, players and the irrepressible Burrell. Another source of tension was the perceived differences between the well-paid British-based professionals and those who eked out a much more paltry living in Jamaica. Throughout Simoes' charismatic approach held the team together, even though by now nerves were beginning to fray.

At the Stade Félix Bollaert in Lens, Jamaica faced Croatia on 14 June. After Mario Stanic scored for the Croatians, Wimbledon's Robbie Earle equalized just on half time with a powerful header. The Reggae Boyz had enjoyed as much possession as the skilful Croatians, and came close to scoring on a couple of other occasions. The second half, alas, was a different story. As Jamaica began to tire, midfielder Robert Prosinecki lobbed the ball over the Jamaican keeper Warren Barrett. Then, after Burton had come agonisingly close to equalizing, Davor Suker settled the game with a 69th minute goal. There was no way back from 3-1 despite the best efforts of substitutes Boyd and Andy Williams.

The next match, against Argentina at Parc des Princes in Paris on 21 June, is one that most Jamaican fans would probably rather forget. Although the Reggae Boyz started with purpose and courage, they were overwhelmed by the technically brilliant South Americans. The first goal came on 32 minutes

Simoes' charismatic approach held the team together, even though by now nerves were beginning to fray.

Above: Jubilation as Robbie Earle finds the net.

Right: A tough tackle from Croatia.

It was with a potent mix of local talent and experienced players from the UK (who, sceptics said, had suddenly discovered Jamaican roots) that Simoes' squad arrived in France. Expectations in Jamaica were sky-high; neutrals wanted the Reggae Boyz to do well simply because they were underdogs and, not least, because they looked like they enjoyed their football. And then there was the atmosphere. Several thousand Jamaicans were in France to support their team, some from the UK and Europe, others from Jamaica itself. They brought a good-natured fanaticism, some loud reggae sound systems (and the

when Ariel Ortega capitalized on Juan Sebastian Veron's through ball. After Derby's Darryl Powell had been sent off in the 46th minute, things did not look promising. In the second half ten-man Jamaica fell apart under the persistent pressure exerted by Argentina. Ortega scored again, then Gabriel Batistuta chalked up a hat-trick, including a penalty. Simoes was telling the truth after the game when he admitted that "we were beaten by the better team". "We do not have the right experience," he added.

Above: The Jamaicans line up before meeting Argentina.

Right: Batistuta scores for Argentina.

If the Jamaicans were deflated by their treatment at the hands of the Argentines, they managed not to show it in their third and final game on 26 June against Japan, also without a point after defeats by Croatia and Argentina. Neither side could therefore qualify for the next round. Perhaps it was because the pressure was effectively off (or because the Japanese were a less formidable proposition than the others) that Jamaica finally began to play.

In front of 24,000 spectators in Lyon, the Japanese started more brightly, but the break came for Jamaica in the 30th minute when Theodore "Tapper" Whitmore fought off two defenders to score with a low shot. In the second half he doubled his tally, and although Masashi Nakayama pulled a goal back, Jamaica held on, with Aaron "Spider" Lawrence forced to make some fine saves

It was redemption of a sort. The Reggae Boyz had won a game at the highest level,

Right: Paul Hall under pressure.

Far right: Following the Reggae Boyz.

"We were beaten by the better team... we do not have the right experience"

Right: Darryl Powell shields the ball.

and the relief was palpable. To have returned beaten three times to Jamaica would have been unbearable, and even though there was a sense of anti-climax among players and coaching staff, there was also pride that a poor country of 2.5 million people had produced a world-class team. If the players did not return to a tumultuous reception, they at least went home with their heads held high.

Below: Walter Boyd gets physical against Japan.

Simoes departed in March 2000 after poor results for Jamaica in the CONCACAF Gold Cup against Colombia and Honduras. He was replaced by fellow Brazilian coach Sebastiao Lazaroni, who lasted six weeks before handing over to another Brazilian Clovis de Oliveira. Then after various reshuffles, Lazaroni was back. In the meantime, Peter Cargill, an influential member of the 1998 Reggae Boyz squad, died tragically in March 2005 in a motor accident. Cargill, by then a coach at Waterhouse FC and a former national under-23 coach, was a pivotal figure in Jamaican football.

Friday 9 December 2005

The draw is made. After a lavish and interminably long ceremony in Leipzig, attended by such luminaries as Pele, Johann Cruyff and German supermodel Heidi Klum, the Soca Warriors know that they must face Paraguay, Sweden and England. In a pub in Staffordshire Christopher Birchall stood nervously with his parents as the red balls were pulled from the different "pots". Lother Matthaus, a former World Cup winner, it was who pulled out the Trinidad & Tobago, bringing a look of delight not only to the face of Leo Beenhakker but also Sven Goran Eriksson. Birchall whooped with delight, as did Trinidadians around the world. It was the dream draw.

Trinidad & Tobago, listed 51st in FIFA's national football rankings, had never played England (9th) or Sweden (14th). But in 1989 the team played Paraguay (30th) in two friendlies, which ended honours even at 2-2 and 1-1. There were few conclusions to be drawn from past form.

The odds on a Trinidad & Tobago victory were, to say the least, long: 1000-1 or more. Even so, the players sounded up-beat. Kelvin Jack told the media that the Soca Warriors were relishing the chance to take on England, while Birchall said that he was living the dream. Optimism was the order of the day, and Dwight Yorke rightly chided US coach Bruce Arena when he numbered Trinidad & Tobago among the no-hope teams.

A wittier take on the situation was offered by Lisana Liburd of the *Trinidad & Tobago Express*, who looked at the consoling notion that at least the team hadn't drawn Brazil:

> *The problem with that idea is that if you are Cyd Gray and you stop the likes of Defence Force striker Bevon Lewis and United Petrotrin Peter Prospect for a living—with all due respect to those two gentlemen—surely there is not much difference whether you face Rooney or Brazil's Ronaldinho or even Sweden's Zlatan Ibrahamovic or Paraguay's Roque Santa Cruz for that matter.*

The odds on a Trinidad & Tobago victory were, to say the least, long: 1000-1 or more.

A good point. But until the whistle blows at 5pm on Saturday 10 June and Trinidad & Tobago face Sweden in Dortmund, players, staff and fans will live the dream. And anyone who underestimates the Soca Warriors will do so at their own peril.

Part Two

Then and Now: A Brief History

It would be nice to prove that football was invented in the Caribbean. After all, the peace-loving indigenous Arawaks, who were wiped out within a few generations of Columbus' arrival in 1492, played a game with a rubber ball in which they apparently were not allowed to use their hands. But was it football? Probably not.

Kick Off

Rather more likely is the accepted view that football—in an organized form—arrived in the Caribbean in the last decade of the nineteenth century with the British. The Trinidad & Tobago Football Association identifies the key date as 1893, the year that Scottish-born Thomas Boyd, a recent arrival in what was then a colony, decided that he wanted a kickabout. One of a large number of Scots who came to work in the sugar and retail sectors, Boyd had played football in his native Scotland. But when he thought that Port of Spain's expansive Savannah would make a good place for a pitch, he realized that there was one slight problem: not a single football existed in Trinidad.

According to historian Valentino Singh, once Boyd's family had sent him a football (plus two spare bladders and an inflator) he was ready to shoo the grazing cows off the Savannah and organize a

Below: Guyanese Amerindians enjoy a kickabout.

game. He may have feared that nobody would show up, but that was far from the case. The *Sports Weekly* wrote, "Thirty persons turned up and sides were formed. Jackets and caps were used as goalposts and the game started. After 15 minutes, most of the players were 'hors de combat,' and declared that the climatic conditions were against the winter sport. The remainder continued to play."

From this no doubt chaotic first game emerged what would become Trinidad & Tobago's football culture. A first club, the British Rovers Club, was formed with Boyd as its captain, and it played regular matches against the only other organized sporting outfit in the island—the Queen's Park Cricket Club. It was probably more interesting when ships called into port, for then the local footballers could test their skills against a team of sailors. The Rovers soon folded, however, but other clubs began to take shape, representing different class and colour groupings within the colony. The Scots, including Boyd, formed Clydesdale. The "poor whites" who had arrived in Trinidad from other smaller Caribbean islands gathered together under the name of the Casuals. Catholics were organized by an Irish priest into Shamrock. These teams were joined by others from the police force and two colleges.

By 1908 the game was deeply enough entrenched for a first football association to be formed. Six entirely amateur teams were involved, and the first match, played on the Savannah, took place on 19 September that year. Clydesdale beat the Casuals by 2-1, and the Sporting Chronicle the next day reported that "the game was interesting, aye, even thrilling". It was also popular with spectators: "Fully half an hour before play began, a very large gathering was seen around the ropes and by 5 p.m.—the opening hour—the attendance was a reward. The fairer sex were not to be denied. They filled the gallery on the north and south boundaries."

Like most things in colonial Trinidad & Tobago, football was liable to be dominated by snobbery and racism. The first teams were exclusively white, and when Majestic, a team for those whom *Sports Weekly* described as "coloured", was formed in 1909, it was not a great success, lacking the money and social status to mount a challenge against the wealthier clubs. Even so, the sport was progressing by leaps and bounds by 1912, when a team from the south of the island, aptly baptized Southern, beat Clydesdale 4-0 in a charity game in Port of Spain. Of the 4,000 fans present, many had journeyed by steamer from the south.

In Jamaica the birth of the sport was broadly similar. The first recorded team, the York Castle school eleven, appears to have

made its debut in 1883 under the watchful eye of Rev. G. C. Hendricks. Thereafter, for the next half century, the island's football was organized around a set of private clubs, which often doubled as cricket clubs. By 1906 there was enough interest in the game for an inaugural meeting of the teams intending to compete for the Martinez Association Football Cup. There were also competitions between schoolboy sides, with trophies donated by such grandees as the former Governor, Sir Sydney Olivier.

The Kingston area was the centre of early Jamaican football, and the Jamaica Football Association, founded in 1910, brought together a number of teams from the Corporate Area such as Railway, YMCA, St. George's Old Boys and Lucas. The presence of a colonial military force was evident in the existence of Army Foreign FC, who competed against Army Local.

The British were also behind the introduction of football into the French territories of Martinique and Guadeloupe. The town of Saint Pierre, tragically destroyed in the great volcanic eruption of 1902, was a frequent port of call for British merchant seamen, and they introduced football into the island in the late nineteenth century. By 1890 a sporting association had been established in Fort-de-France, with the first football club formed in the same city in 1903. In Guadeloupe the sport's origins were very similar, and early players were a mix of foreign sailors, French-born civil servants and Guadeloupeans who had experienced the sport in Europe. In French Guiana, however, it was Brazilians rather than British who were behind football's early development, with a league set up by 1912.

Meanwhile, in Cuba the first recorded football match took place on 11 December 1911 between Sport Club Hatuey, seemingly mostly comprised of Spanish-born or descended players, and the very British-sounding Rovers Athletic Club, whose line-up

included names such as Jack Orr, P. J. Thompson and D. Tucker. Rovers won by a goal to nil, scored by Orr.

The Bahamas embraced football in the years following the First World War, when returning soldiers carried on playing the sport they had discovered in Britain. By the 1920s there were regular organized games between sides in New Providence, with visiting British naval ships providing occasional opposition.

Haiti, for its part, was a comparative latecomer to organized football, largely because the island was in a state of almost permanent political turmoil at the beginning of the twentieth century when other Caribbean territories were discovering the sport. Even so, a federation was formed in 1904, but there seem to have been few, if any, recorded matches. In 1915 a series of violent insurrections led the US government to invade Haiti, and the Marines stayed there until 1934. During that time there was little in the way of structured football, but interestingly, Haitians never took to baseball in the same way as the people of the neighbouring Dominican Republic, which was also occupied by the US between 1916 and 1924.

By 1925 Haiti was in a position to organize a national team, which took on Jamaica in a three-match series in Port-au-Prince. The Jamaicans won all three games, and then went on to trounce their opponents 6-0 in a return game at Sabina Park.

Below: St. Kitts national side, 1951-52, Leeward Islands champions.

From Strength to Strength

Football gradually consolidated itself throughout the Caribbean from the 1920s onwards, but always had to struggle either against cricket in the English-speaking territories, or baseball elsewhere. Football associations were founded in Suriname (1920) the Netherlands Antilles (1921), Grenada (1924), Cuba (1924) Antigua & Barbuda (1928), Bermuda (1928), St. Kitts & Nevis (1932) and Aruba (1932). These associations joined the already established organizations in Trinidad & Tobago, Jamaica, Haiti, British Guiana (1902) and Barbados (1910). Others would come later, such as the Bahamas in 1967, Dominica (1970) and St. Lucia and St. Vincent & the Grenadines (1979).

The sport at this period was exclusively amateur and largely run by schoolmasters, churchmen and local philanthropists. Clubs represented distinct localities, and there was little or no movement of players between them. Clubs could be organized along parish or village lines, and there were also some that represented large workplaces or professions. The long-lasting influence of Britain on the game was tangible in the names of some clubs: Arsenal Football Club in Haiti were unbeaten champions in the 1943 season, while other islands paid tribute to clubs like Everton or Burnley with their local team names. In Trinidad Everton, a mostly black team from rough and tough inner-city Port of Spain rose to prominence in the 1930s, beating more genteel sides such as the Casuals despite the fact that they had no clubhouse and were largely unpaid.

Football had to struggle against cricket in the English-speaking territories, or baseball elsewhere

For most players the opportunity to make a real impression took place only rarely when international friendlies were staged. The four big footballing nations—Cuba, Haiti, Jamaica and Trinidad & Tobago—mainly played among themselves from the 1940s up to the 1960s, although occasionally teams from Central America or the Dutch Caribbean colonies would provide the opposition. One exception to the general rule took place in 1952, when the Jamaica Football Association organized a three-game series between the national team and the so-called Caribbean All Stars, a collection of players from Cuba, Haiti, Suriname, British Guiana, Puerto Rico,

Below: Well-dressed football crowd, Kingston, 1920s.

Above: Castro demonstrates how to kick a ball.

Guadeloupe and Trinidad & Tobago. Jamaica's two British-based stars, "Lindy" Delapenha and Giles Heron were on hand to help the home side edge the context, with Jamaica winning 2-1 and 1-0 and losing 1-5. The series, set up to provide much-needed financial relief in the wake of a hurricane, was the brainchild of the newly formed Caribbean Football Association, formed by representatives from Trinidad & Tobago, Guadeloupe, Suriname, British Guiana, Jamaica, the Dominican Republic, Haiti and Puerto Rico.

Despite its presence in these regional competitions, Cuba was hardly a football-mad nation, as baseball held a tight grip on sporting life. Even so, its historic and cultural links with the footballing republics of Central America led it, only months after Fidel Castro's revolution, to host a Central American Championship in Havana in February 1960. The baseball-loving Castro inaugurated proceedings with a powerful toe-poke.

An important development in 1963 was the founding of CONCACAF, the Confederación Centroamerica y del Caribe de Fútbol, an umbrella organization aimed at bringing together the football associations of the Caribbean and Central America into a single grouping. Controlled and funded by FIFA, the Swiss-based world football organization, CONCACAF at first had a low profile, but would later play a vital role in the region's football.

Even as football began to take off across the region, few players were making any money from their endeavours. Indeed, some quite literally turned up to play in bare feet. In 1946, for instance, the players representing SV Robinhood in Suriname were awarded a dozen pairs of boots for winning their league (boots were a condition for playing in the second division of the Suriname national league).

The Jamaica Football Federation's history relates how until the 1960s players in the national team were expected to turn up with their own boots and shorts, while officials would make sure that all shirts and socks loaned to the team were returned at the end of the game. After one match in 1951 the Jamaican players were reportedly handed an envelope each—which turned out to contain only a thank-you note. The JFF remarks:

> *However, they never failed to give unqualified dedication to the team. Through it all, Pinkie Smith would row his boat from his home in Port Royal, dock at King Street, jog to Sabina Park, play for Jamaica and return home by the same route.*

Amateurish in the best sense it may have been, but by the 1960s Jamaica was turning out players of serious quality such as midfielder Syd Bartlett and strikers Lascelles Dunkley and Oscar Black. In 1962 the Jamaica Football Federation replaced the JFA and was accepted as a full member by FIFA. The same year, the year of Jamaica's independence, the 35,000-capacity National Stadium in Kingston (fondly known as "the Office") was inaugurated. Suddenly, the game was being taken more seriously by the new administration.

Then, in 1965, under the leadership of Brazilian coach Jorge Penna, Jamaica made a spirited first attempt to qualify for World Cup finals—to be held in England in 1966. After overcoming Cuba and the Netherlands Antilles in the first round, the team faced stiffer opposition in the form of Mexico and Costa Rica. The first game against Mexico was a narrow 2-3 defeat; the return match in Mexico City, in front of an intimidating crowd of 52,000, was a rout. Jamaica lost 8-0, largely because the team had arrived at 9 a.m. on the day of the match and played, at high altitude, at midday. They then lost 7-0 away to Costa Rica before drawing 1-1 with the Central Americans in Kingston.

Trinidad & Tobago, meanwhile, became a full member of FIFA in 1964 and, like Jamaica,

...few players were making any money from their endeavours.

started to modernize its approach to football. The first real evidence of improvement came three years later when the country sent a team to participate in the Pan-American Games in Winnipeg, Canada. Not only did the Trinidadians beat Colombia 5-2, but they even took on and defeated mighty Argentina 1-0, with a goal from Kelvin Berassa. Perhaps at that stage their self-confidence ran a little too high, for when they met Bermuda in the semi-final they went down 3-1. But in the final match against Canada honour was more than salvaged as Trinidad & Tobago ran out 4-1 winners and won the competition's bronze medal.

Black Power

From the 1930s through to independence in the 1960s, the Caribbean was a region of divided societies, in which the black majority struggled to realize its political and economic aspirations against those of a small, lighter-skinned, financially powerful minority. Riots and demonstrations were a regular feature of this period, but social tensions were also reflected on the football pitch.

Some clubs, as we have seen, started by operating a colour bar, and if this became less obvious as time went on, it was still the case that many of the region's more up-market clubs were the preserve of the well-heeled minority. Football may have been liked by the masses, but it was mostly played, at club level at least, by people who could afford their own boots. Clubs were funded by local businesses or wealthy individuals, and although no players were paid they had to conform to the middle-class attitudes of their patrons.

But in the period following the Second World War, as Britain sought to end its colonial presence in the Caribbean and reform was in the air, new structures emerged to meet the needs of the majority of footballers and fans. In Trinidad & Tobago new leagues were formed in rural areas, and the descendants of indentured labourers from India and China formed their own teams. In the urban areas in and around Port of Spain teams that followed in the footsteps of Everton and reflected local communities began to take shape, challenging the dominance of the more genteel clubs of former times. Old-established sides like Shamrock gradually faded away. Black administrators started to take important positions in the hierarchy of the sport. Under the aegis of Jack Warner, newly appointed secretary of the Trinidad & Tobago Football Association, a National Football League was formed in 1974, offering a more

representative contest between teams from all over the two islands.

Growing assertiveness on the part of players sometimes led to confrontation. In 1970, for instance, while Trinidad was reeling from the impact of the "Black Power" rebellion and near mutiny, the country was host to a six-nation CONCACAF tournament. The Trinidad & Tobago players suddenly threatened to go on strike unless their demands were met: two pairs of boots, insurance, track suits, four complimentary passes, hotel accommodation, compensation for lack of earnings, TT$500 expenses, and a tour of Canada if successful. The threat eventually blew over, but it illustrated the low expectations of local players as well as their growing sense of self-worth.

In Jamaica, Penna's attempt to forge a credible national team had involved recruiting players from some of the tougher inner-city districts of Kingston. As in Trinidad & Tobago,

These teams were a far cry from those patronized by the colonial elite in the 1930s.

clubs were formed in the 1960s and 1970s that were strongly rooted in urban communities, particularly in the poorer areas of the capital. Harbour View FC dates from the 1960s, while Arnett Gardens FC was formed in 1977 in a merger between Jones Town and All Saints teams. Tivoli Gardens FC, named after the "ghetto" district of West Kingston, and Boy's Town FC are other clubs formed at around this time.

These teams were a far cry from those patronized by the colonial elite in the 1930s. They attracted fanatical support from people living in the communities where they were

There was never any doubt that the Caribbean could produce top-quality players.

based, and they reinforced the fierce rivalries that already existed between these communities. In the 1970s and 1980s party politics in Jamaica divided Kingston's low-income districts into warring "garrisons", where partisan activism often took the form of shoot-outs and stabbings. The two political parties each had their "dons" or local barons, who distributed money, favours and weapons in return for loyalty. Not surprisingly, football was drawn into this dangerous cocktail of political violence. A match between Tivoli Gardens and Waterhouse, linked respectively with the two major parties, was no place for the casual onlooker.

In the bad years Jamaican football was scarred by indiscipline and aggression of all sorts. Crowd trouble was commonplace, as were assaults on players, referees and linesmen. Bottles were thrown, knives brandished, shots fired. Predictably, these alarming events discouraged many ordinary Jamaicans from attending games. They also deterred sponsors and other investors from pumping money into the game. And money was very much what Jamaican—and other Caribbean—football needed at the time: for facilities, training and safety, let alone players' wages.

Significantly, the most popular competition in Jamaica at this time was the Manning Cup, contested between the island's secondary schools. This competition was less tainted by thuggery than any other football event, and drew large crowds, especially to the final. Another well-supported competition was the Olivier Shield, also contested by college teams. Many of the most promising

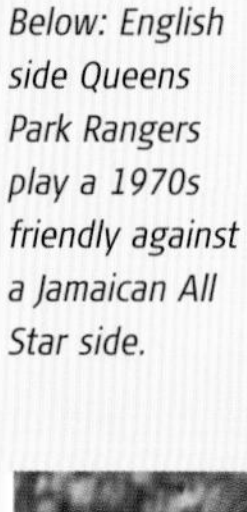

Below: English side Queens Park Rangers play a 1970s friendly against a Jamaican All Star side.

boys who played high school football would later be tempted abroad, primarily to the USA, by the prospect of college scholarships.

There was also occasional light relief in the form of friendlies between local sides and visiting teams from Britain, Europe or South America.

Leading from the Front

There was never any doubt that the Caribbean could produce top-quality players. The problems in the 1970s and 1980s were more ones of organization and resources. With inadequate government and private investment, grounds and facilities were mostly ramshackle. There was not enough money to create youth training structures or to provide the infrastructure for developing strong national sides. Trinidad & Tobago's near miss in the qualifying rounds of the 1974 World Cup underlined that the nation had talent in abundance but also revealed how it could be derailed—in this case by spectacularly incompetent refereeing.

Above: Manning Cup action.

Below: Pele (in white suit) poses with Gally Cummings and others during the 1972 Santos tour of Trinidad & Tobago.

In the 1990s Caribbean football really came of age, particularly in Jamaica and Trinidad & Tobago, as two highly ambitious and often controversial figures took over the reigns of the sport's administration. In Jamaica, Captain Horace Burrell, a retired army officer and owner of a successful bakery business, was elected president of the Jamaica Football Federation in 1994.

Burrell was already vice-president of the Caribbean Football Union, founded in 1978, and active on FIFA and CONCACAF disciplinary committees, and was hence well connected in the world of international football administration. His business interests also allowed him to invest

some of his own money into the island's football federation as well as enabling him to make the most of other corporate investment.

As the Reggae Boyz' bid to reach the 1998 World Cup finals, under the inspirational management of Rene Simoes, gathered pace, so businesses began to get behind the sport, effectively paying the national team's wages during the latter stages of the competition. Burrell was instrumental in attracting this essential financial support as well as winning the backing of the government. His efforts to propel the national side towards success were not always appreciated; his style could appear abrasive and there were well-documented episodes of confrontation between the JFF president and the coaching staff and players. Money, in particular, was always an issue, as the JFF sought to cover its expenses and pay the high costs of running a World Cup campaign, while the players—reasonably enough—expected significant remuneration for their efforts.

In the event, the Jamaican adventure in the 1998 World Cup failed to meet with the hoped-for outcome, but Burrell had done a great deal to raise the profile of the game among the business community as well as ordinary fans. It was noted by many that Jamaica's extraordinarily high crime rate dipped spectacularly during the World Cup finals. This achievement, however, did not prevent Burrell from losing his re-election campaign in late 2003, although he clearly remains an important figure in Jamaican football.

Jack Warner, the driving force behind Trinidadian football, is an even more formidable committee man and administrator than Burrell. His involvement in the nation's footballing affairs dates back to the early 1970s, and since then he has risen to be president of CONCACAF and vice-president of FIFA. With the help of these well-paid jobs, Warner has considerable interests in real estate and hotels in Trinidad as well as owning local team Joe Public FC.

Known as a local "godfather", who will often spend his own money on advancing the cause of national football, Warner has not been afraid to court controversy and to make enemies, not least because of his high political profile. His power within the FIFA hierarchy is immense, as he effectively controls the 35 or so Caribbean votes in the organization's decision-making council. (Under FIFA rules an affiliate like Montserrat or the US Virgin Islands has the same voting clout as Brazil or England.) As such, Warner's influence in world football is considerable. He has faced many allegations of impropriety over the years, not least in regard to the allocation of tickets for the 2006 World Cup finals and his own interests in a tour operator, but has weathered the storms.

His business acumen, however, is beyond dispute and has been amply demonstrated by his years at the helm of CONCACAF. Warner took the post of president after Trinidad & Tobago's traumatic near-qualification in 1989, inheriting a near-bankrupt organization based in the regional backwater of Guatemala City. He soon managed to improve the organization's profile, masterminding its move to headquarters in New York City. Wooing such big-name sponsors as Coca-Cola and Budweiser, Warner capitalized on the growing popularity of football—or soccer—in the USA, particularly when FIFA handed the 1994 World Cup finals to the Americans. "I was able to see," he said, "that football and business are not enemies."

Above: The 1989 Trinidad & Tobago side, a.k.a. the Strike Squad.

Right: Jack Warner meets Kofi Annan, Zurich, February 2006.

...businesses began to get behind the sport, effectively paying the national team's wages.

If Warner's ambitions for Trinidad & Tobago football were frustrated by the near-misses of 1973 and 1989, he was determined that the 2006 campaign should not repeat history. So it was that he was involved in the management shake-up that brought Leo Beenhakker into the coach's role as well as in the push to goad government and the private sector into helping to fund the campaign. With the full weight of his CONCACAF and FIFA status behind him, Warner was an unstoppable force behind the Soca Warriors.

With qualification to the 2006 finals assured, the sponsorship money began to roll in, much to Warner's delight. A US$11.5-million deal with Adidas followed announcements from local brewers, Carib, and KFC among others that they would be supporting the Germany campaign.

Professionalism

For almost all of its history, Caribbean football has been the preserve of the amateur. Players have, of course, been paid in various ways by those with the means to do so, either through prize money, gifts or other inducements. But the professional footballer, earning a regular monthly salary and doing nothing else but play football, has hardly ever existed in the region.

Given the lack of resources, the unwillingness of business to support the sport and the inability of many fans to pay for anything other than cheap tickets, this is hardly surprising. When clubs in the English premiership amass debts of millions of pounds and American football leagues go bankrupt, it is clear that football—aside from the likes of Manchester United, Barcelona and Juventus—can be a highly unprofitable business. And in the Caribbean, where millionaire backers and wealthy fan bases are thin on the ground, the prospects for successful professional football are unpromising. Indeed, in the smaller islands the idea of professional football is simply unfeasible. Only in Jamaica and Trinidad & Tobago might it take shape.

Many within the sport are adamant that only professional structures in Caribbean football will raise the standard of the game, draw bigger crowds and sponsors, and prevent the drain of players overseas. A statement by Harbour View FC, one of Jamaica's leading clubs, makes the point that Jamaica cannot compete with the likes of the USA, Mexico and Canada, which all have professional leagues. "If Jamaica is to become a consistent qualifier in the various world championships full professional football must be established by way of a professional

Right: Premier League football, Jamaica.

Below right: A Wray & Nephew league clash.

Below: Joe Public, Trinidad.

league... A football industry properly structured will increase employment and become a net foreign currency earner. We are no longer purely recreational; we certainly provide major entertainment."

As things stand in Jamaica, the Wray & Nephews Premier League is mostly semi-professional, with the majority of players, coaches and staff receiving some payment. Waterhouse FC, situated in one of Kingston's tough inner-city areas and a ferocious rival to Tivoli Gardens, was reported to have received J$24 million (US$400,000) in sponsorship in 2003 and is believed to have an annual budget of J$16 million (US$250,000), including wages. Some players might earn J$100,000 (US$1,500) per month, a derisory sum by British standards but an acceptable wage in Jamaica. Transparency is not a prominent feature of Caribbean club football, so it is difficult to ascertain what payments are made to whom, but it seems likely that at least the biggest Jamaican clubs—Harbour View, Waterhouse, Arnett Gardens, etc.—pay at least some players on a regular basis.

In Trinidad & Tobago the T & T Pro League is country's premier division. Set up in 1999 as the Professional Football League, it has struggled from the outset, faced by public apathy and financial constraints. While most clubs are dependent on corporate sponsors, few can rely on any meaningful income from gate money. Critics have pointed out that professional football will only prosper in Trinidad & Tobago if clubs have a strong local identity and following. As it is, teams like Defence Force and Police have little popular support outside their particular professions. Other clubs have some local following, but even their names—W Connection, Joe Public—do not reflect a sense of place.

We are no longer purely recreational; we provide major entertainment.

Valentino Singh's history of the island's football suggests that attempts to set up professional structures in Trinidad & Tobago have always been bedevilled by schisms, financial difficulties and issues of personal ego. As far back as 1981, a local businessman called Arthur Suite attempted to launch what he called the Trinidad & Tobago Premier Soccer League. In it were various teams including his own Aviation Services Ltd. (ASL), and he offered TT$160,000 of prize money to the winners as well as paying the ASL players. This league, which Warner at the Trinidad & Tobago Football Association promptly tried to ban, then mutated into the Carib Professional League, competing with the Stag National Football League. The two rival leagues finally amalgamated in 1983.

Nor were later bids to form a single national league any more straightforward. When in 2002 Jack Warner withdrew his support from the Professional Football League, professional football was close to collapse until Larry Romany and a group of club chairmen salvaged the league under the new T & T Pro League identity. Sponsored by several businesses and with some modest government backing, the T &T pro League brings together seven clubs, including Tobago United.

Professional players in Trinidad can expect as little as TT$2,000 (US$320) monthly (the PFL-approved minimum was actually slashed from TT$2,000 to TT$1200 in 2002). When that year Jack Warner withdrew his team, Joe Public FC, from the PFL, he pointed out that players were earning between TT$4,000 (US$640) and TT$7,500 (US$1,200) monthly. Joe Public's 2002 withdrawal from the league and move to the rival Sportsworld National Super League further emphasized the problems—financial and political—facing Trinidad & Tobago's professional footballers. Little wonder that one of the main concerns of local players looking forward to the 2006 World Cup finals was that they should be properly remunerated. All too often in the past, they have not been.

Right: After the match, St. Kitts.

Below: Football ground at Montego Bay, Jamaica.

Across the Region

Professional football may be the Holy Grail of Caribbean football, but its day-to-day lifeblood is the amateur ethos—a love of the sport and a desire to represent village, youth club or school. All across the region, teams of all ages and backgrounds are organized into leagues, sometimes sponsored by local businesses or more reliant on the goodwill of individuals. The smaller islands such as Anguilla or the Turks & Caicos Islands may have but a handful of local teams; the bigger territories of Trinidad & Tobago have competitions organized at parish and local level as well as national leagues.

Facilities vary widely. Some of the region's bigger clubs have proper grounds, with floodlighting, covered seating and a good pitch. Smaller teams play at rudimentary

venues, where pitches can be rock hard or muddy depending on the weather. Village games are often played in the most rural settings, with sugar-cane fields and palm trees creating the scenery. There is little funding, from government or private sector, for major ground development, and what money comes to local football associations from FIFA is more usually invested in coaching, training referees and encouraging school-level football.

Professional football may be the Holy Grail of Caribbean football, but its day-to-day lifeblood is the amateur ethos

The greatest challenge for many Caribbean footballers is to face competition from overseas, and inter-Caribbean rivalry is fierce. All teams, whether school-based or local, itch to play their counterparts from other islands. This dimension of regional football takes place at club level with the prestigious CONCACAF Champions' Cup, in which teams within the Caribbean compete in the Caribbean Football Union contest, with the winner going forward to take on the Central American and North American champions. The final prize is entry into the FIFA Club World Championship. The CONCACAF Champions' Cup, which started in 1962, has been won by clubs from Haiti (1963 and 1984), Suriname (1981) and Trinidad & Tobago's Defence Force (1985). In December 2005 Portmore United FC of Jamaica overcame Robinhood of Suriname to progress to the next round.

At national level, apart from the regular CONCACAF World Cup qualifying rounds (which for some smaller teams are often restricted to two preliminary games) there is the Digicel Caribbean Cup, which replaced the earlier Copa Caribe and Shell Caribbean Cup in 2005 when the telecommunications company decided to sponsor it. This is a biannual tournament among Caribbean Football Union federations, with the top three teams winning a place in the CONCACAF Gold Cup. This, in turn, is a bigger contest, bringing together winners from North and Central America as well as the Caribbean. In 2005 Jamaica won the Digicel trophy plus US$100,000, beating Cuba 1-0 in the final held in Barbados. In the following CONCACAF Gold Cup in the USA Jamaica made it to the quarter finals before being knocked out by the host nation.

Above: St. Kitts' Orville Thompson scores his national side's first goal in the Shell Caribbean Cup against French Guiana, 1989.

Left: Trump Tower, New York, CONCACAF's headquarters.

CONCACAF

Apart from the World Cup the CONCACAF Gold Cup is the biggest target for all Caribbean teams. Held every two years, it pits the Caribbean sides against bigger international players such as Mexico and the USA. Renamed the Gold Cup in 1991 in order to appeal to a growing US audience, it has since been dominated by the Americans and Mexicans. It was in 1973 that a Caribbean team, Haiti, last won the competition, thereby earning a place in the 1974 World Cup finals.

One of CONCACAF's showpiece events, the Gold Cup reflects the huge part played by the organization in regional football. From its unpromising beginnings in Guatemala City, CONCACAF (also known as the Football Confederation) has grown to become a major part of FIFA's world outreach and an influential player in the politics of football. Those who walk the corridors of power inside CONCACAF's New York's Trump Tower offices earn lavish salaries and have a decisive impact on football throughout the Caribbean. The world they inhabit is a million miles from the day-to-day reality of small-island football, where resources are often critically limited.

The Gold Cup reflects the huge part played by CONCACAF in regional football

CONCACAF's growth has been spectacular, mainly fuelled by accelerating interest in football in the USA, with a corresponding rise in revenue from TV rights, attendances and merchandising. The fact that two CONCACAF-affiliated nations—the USA and Mexico—are ranked in FIFA's top ten gives the organization more credibility than it had twenty years ago. It also generates a great deal of money: the Gold Cup brought in eight times more revenue in 2005 than in its first year, 1991. This, according to General Secretary Chuck Blazer, funds all other competitions organized by CONCACAF and many development programmes.

CONCACAF also receives millions of dollars annually from FIFA to support regional football and football associations. From FIFA, too, comes the Goal programme, set up by

Below: Haseley Crawford Stadium, Port of Spain.

FIFA president Sepp Blatter, as a way of channelling resources to the world's poorest footballing nations. In recent years many Caribbean football associations, from the Bahamas and Montserrat to the Netherlands Antilles and Dominica, have received grants from Goal, enabling them to build or refurbish headquarters, improve pitches and training facilities and strengthen the game generally.

CONCACAF's growth has been spectacular, mainly fuelled by accelerating interest in football in the USA

Above: Futsal.

Right: Jamaican women's team triumphant.

New Directions

One of CONCACAF's most positive contributions to the sport has been its active promotion of women's football. For many decades, of course, Caribbean football was an all-male preserve and a bastion of chauvinism. As early as 1923 a women's match had taken place at the St. James barracks in Port of Spain, but the *Sporting Chronicle* took a dim view of the event:

> *Our morals must not yet descend to any such level. There are many other games such as tennis, golf, cricket etc. which our young ladies might do well to take up. The very idea of women in football attire should be a deterrent to feminists taking up such a pastime. May it never occur again.*

Times change, and since the 1980s a growing interest in the sport on the part of women, together with increasing resources, has brought a spectacular increase in female participation at every level and in every territory. Even some countries with no real track record in men's football have produced women's teams of considerable promise. In October 2005, for instance, the Dominican Republic—hardly a big name in international football—fielded a side against the British Virgin Islands in the FIFA U-20 Women's World Championship. The Dominicans won by a record margin of 25-0, with Osama Valerio scoring a personal record of ten goals.

Not all women's contests are so one-sided. While the CONCACAF big-name teams like the USA and Mexico have strong women's sides, so too do Jamaica, Haiti and Trinidad & Tobago. The CONCACAF qualifying games that eventually lead to an appearance at the Olympic Games are particularly hard-fought. In 2004 the USA and Mexico went through to the Athens finals.

Locally, almost every Caribbean territory hosts a women's competition. In the tiny Turks & Caicos Islands, for example, five teams compete against each other, with Horizon FC battling for supremacy with Turquoise FC. In Jamaica the women's teams tend to be affiliated to the established semi-professional clubs, with familiar names like Harbour View, Waterhouse and Portmore leading the field. In Trinidad & Tobago, meanwhile, where the international women's team is rated 39th in the world, league football is less impressive, with only a handful of good teams and a short two-month season.

The growth in women's football has been paralleled by an explosion of interest in futsal, "Futbal-Salsa", an indoor five-a-side variation of football that originated in South America in the 1930s. With the emphasis on closer control and individual skill rather than stamina, this game has wide appeal across Latin America, where it is the preferred training game for professionals and others. The Caribbean has not been slow to take to futsal, particularly in the Spanish-speaking territories of Cuba, Puerto Rico and the Dominican Republic where traditional football is less entrenched.

FIFA and CONCACAF organize competitions for men and women at differing age levels, while the indefatigable Jack Warner has been instrumental in finding funding for purpose-built futsal facilities in Trinidad & Tobago. Although in its infancy compared to football itself, futsal may yet be the way to attract future generations to the Beautiful Game.

One of CONCACAF's positive contributions to the sport has been its active promotion of women's football

John Barnes in his Liverpool days.
Right: SS Empire Windrush arrives in Tilbury, 1948.

Part Three

Foreign Legionaries: Caribbean Footballers Abroad

How many promising footballers were aboard, one wonders, when the SS *Empire Windrush* moored at Tilbury docks on 22 June 1948? The ship had carried 492 Jamaicans across the Atlantic to the "mother country". It was the first instalment of what was to be a massive migration of people from the Caribbean into the United Kingdom, a process that lasted until well into the 1960s. Most migrants were in search of work in Britain's post-war economy, where there were plenty of opportunities in manufacturing and public services. They brought with them their own culture, which was to contribute enormously to the development of a multi-cultural Britain. They would also, over time, make a big difference to British football.

Players born in the Caribbean continue to seek their fortune in the British game, as they do in France and elsewhere in Europe. They are joined by ever-increasing numbers of footballers descended from Caribbean migrants, who have been born in the country where they ply their trade. Together they have changed the face of the European game. Some play for Caribbean national sides; others, born in Europe, have represented their countries of birth. In the modern game the two-way traffic of players between the Caribbean and Europe (and to a lesser extent) North America is yet another example of globalization.

Below: Andrew Watson, back row, third from left, a trailblazer. (Scottish Football Museum)

Pioneers

It was long assumed that the first Caribbean-born players to appear in British football arrived in the immediate post-war period, even though there had been isolated examples of black British or British-African footballers before then. But recent research has uncovered the startling fact that Andrew Watson, born in 1857 in the colony of British Guiana, was playing for the amateur Glasgow team Queen's Park FC in the 1880s, also appearing for London Swifts in 1882. Considered an outstanding talent, Watson won two Scottish Cup medals before working

for Queen's Park as club secretary. He pre-dated Walter Tull, born in Folkestone of Barbadian parentage (his grandfather had been a slave) in 1888, who played in midfield for Tottenham Hotspur and Northampton Town from 1909 to the outbreak of the First World War. Lieutenant Tull was killed in action in 1918, but will be remembered for his skills and for the dignity with which he faced racist abuse from supporters of Bristol City. As one observer of the incident in 1909 put it:

> *Let me tell those Bristol hooligans that Tull is so clean in mind and method as to be a model for all white men who play football whether they be amateur or professional. In point of ability, if not actual achievement, Tull was the best forward on the field.*

More Caribbean players came after the Second World War. Born in Kingston in 1922, striker Giles or "Gillie" Heron was signed by Scottish giants Celtic in 1951, scoring on his debut against Morton. While popularly known as "the black flash" for his speed, he was also criticized by the local media for an apparent lack of aggression ("lacking resource when challenged").

"Tull is so clean in mind and method as to be a model for all white men who play football..."

More successful was Lloyd "Lindy" Delapenha, who was born in Kingston in 1927. An outstanding sporting all-rounder, Delapenha was spotted by a football scout while serving in the British army in Egypt in the aftermath of the Second World War. The scout sent him to Arsenal, where he was turned down, and from there he went to Portsmouth where he was signed almost immediately. He played 44 league games for Portsmouth, and was involved in the club's historic league championship victory in 1949 before being sold to Middlesborough for the princely sum of £6,000.

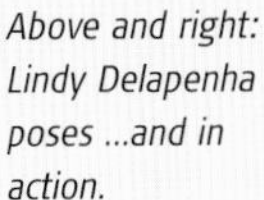

Above and right: Lindy Delapenha poses ...and in action.

It was on Teesside that Delapenha really made his name. Over almost ten years he made 260 league appearances, scoring 90 goals. In a retrospective article of 1991 the *Middlesborough Evening Gazette* recalled: "He had one of the hardest shots of any Boro player and scored many of his goals before the goalkeeper could move. He scored 100 goals in 300 appearances and in the 1953-54 season, he was the top scorer with 18 goals." For this Delapenha was paid £12 per week, with a £2 bonus for a win and £1 for a draw. He eventually returned to Jamaica in 1964 and enjoyed a successful career as a radio commentator and presenter.

From Bermuda came Arnold Woollard, who was spotted by the director of Third Division outfit Northampton Town, and who made his debut for that side in 1949 before being transferred to Peterborough and then mighty Newcastle United. He did not make many first team appearances, but as a reliable full-back was part of the award-winning squad of 1955. Woollard moved again to Bournemouth, then back to Northampton, where he retired in 1963.

Delapenha, Woollard and Heron were the pioneers in what became a better-trodden path from the 1960s onwards. Up until then the vast majority of professional footballers at every level in Britain were white. But gradually this situation began to change, as players from the Caribbean came to play professional football and the sons of Caribbean migrants fought their way through the ranks.

Clyde Best and the Three Degrees

One of the greatest and most influential of this new wave of footballer was Bermuda-born Clyde Best, who signed for West Ham United in 1969. He had already won a cap for Bermuda at the age of fifteen, and inspirational West Ham manager Ron Greenwood was tipped off about this young prodigy. For the next five seasons he was a high-profile member of a squad that included World Cup legends Bobby Moore and Geoff Hurst. A pacy forward with an eye for goal, Best scored 47 goals in 188 appearances for West Ham, endearing himself to the Hammers faithful. In 1997, having lived for many years in California, he finally returned to Bermuda, where he became the Bermudan national coach before returning to work in the Prison Service.

One of Best's many achievements was

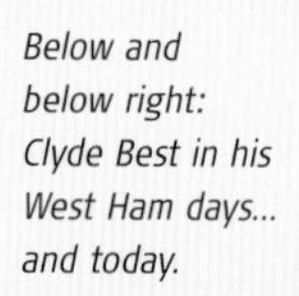

Below and below right: Clyde Best in his West Ham days... and today.

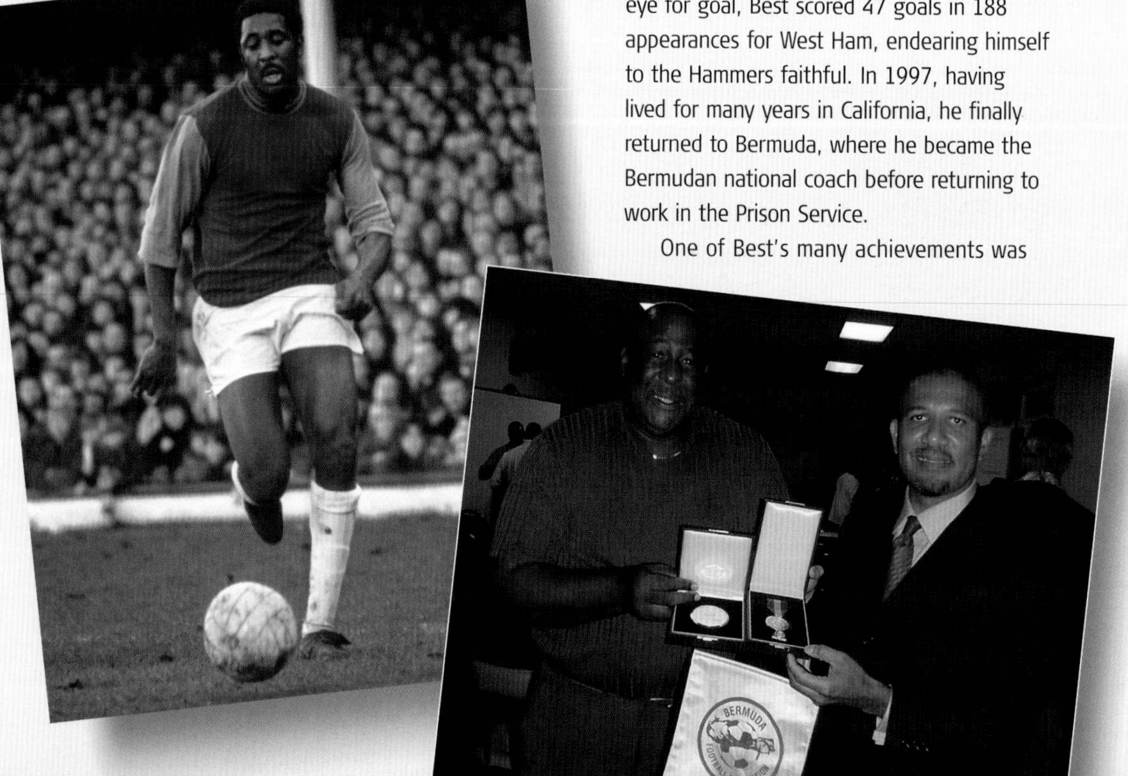

that he rose above the racism that greeted the early black players in Britain. A 2000 article on Soccernet retraced those trials and his response to them:

> *He remembered how they would scream "nigger" at him on the terraces, but he would tell himself "You've got to be mentally strong. Ignore them. Carry yourself in the right manner. Show them the soccer ball doesn't care what colour you are. Give your answer by sticking one in the back of their net."*
>
> *And he did. Forty-seven times in 188 games. He was a lovely, graceful player and even if some felt he underachieved, of course he hadn't. His impact as the first black footballer to imprint himself on the national consciousness in football's TV era could never be measured by goals alone.*

Best was a high-profile member of a squad that included World Cup legends Bobby Moore and Geoff Hurst

Best's presence on the national scene was instrumental in encouraging a generation of young, black, British-born players to believe that they could also break through what had often been seen as the barrier of race. One such footballer recalled: "When I was younger there weren't any black players. I saw that football was dominated by white players and just run by white clubs, and stuff, and when I saw Clyde Best for the first time on TV as a black player it made me think, 'Black men can get into the Football League if they work hard

Below: Brendon Batson challenges Wolves' Jim McCalliog, Highbury, 1973.

adidas

enough at it.'" Fittingly, Clyde Best was awarded the MBE in the 2006 New Year's Honours list for services to football.

"...all we could think of was "we've got to win" ...the racial abuse we had acted as a spur to us..."

Best was followed by several other Caribbean footballers over the next few years. Brendon Batson, who was born in St. George's, Grenada, in 1953, moved to London as a schoolboy and was apparently told by one teacher that he should be playing cricket rather than football. Ignoring this advice, he signed for Arsenal, moved on to Cambridge City and then joined West Bromwich Albion in 1978 for a fee of £30,000. For the next six years, Batson was a regular fixture at Albion, playing 172 times as a cultured full-back. Injury finished his playing career in 1984 and he went on to play a distinguished part in the development of the sport through the Professional Footballers' Association.

Batson was at the time one of a triumvirate of black players at West Bromwich Albion, known affectionately to their fans as "the Three Degrees" and nurtured by then manager Ron Atkinson (who, ironically, later became involved in a notorious allegation of racism when he criticized Marcel Desailly in insulting language in 2004). Laurie Cunningham, who was born in London and started playing with Leyton Orient, was a dazzlingly fast attacker who in 1979 moved to Real Madrid for almost £1 million—the first Englishmen to do so. The third was Cyrille Regis, born in French Guiana of a St. Lucian father in 1958. He also came to London as a boy and there he worked his way through schoolboy and amateur leagues before being spotted by an Albion scout. Between 1977 and 1984 Regis made 302 appearances for the club, scoring a total of 112 goals. He also played five senior games and several Under 21 internationals for England.

Like Clyde Best, the Three Degrees had to confront the worst aspects of British football culture. Batson tells of how at one away game he went out on the pitch to warm up:

> *All I could see was a lot of bananas coming towards me and I thought "how do you react to that?" So I picked one up, peeled it and pretended to eat it. I threw one to Cyrille, he stuck it down his shorts, and we volleyed a few back into the crowd. But all we could think of was "we've got to win this game" and a lot of times the racial abuse we had actually acted as a spur to us giving a good performance. We were just interested in winning the game.*

The Second Wave

Once Best, Batson and Regis had blazed the trail for black footballers in Britain, others followed. Some were of African origin, like young Nigerian Ade Coker, who made an explosive debut for West Ham against Crystal Palace in 1971, replacing the injured Geoff Hurst, and scored a spectacular goal after seven minutes. Others were British-born, like Viv Anderson from Nottingham, the first black footballer ever to represent England in 1978 in a 1-0 victory over Czechoslovakia. Anderson, who was capped thirty times in all,

Left: Cyrille Regis.

posts at Barnsley and Middlesborough.

By the 1980s black players were a relatively common sight at British professional games. By the late 1970s there were reckoned to be some fifty black professionals in Britain. Vince "the Prince" Hilaire was a talented winger who started with Crystal Palace before moving on to Portsmouth and Leeds. Garth Crooks, now a successful media personality, was born in Stoke-on-Trent to Jamaican parents and played for his local team before winning several cups with the successful Tottenham team of the 1980s.

was a swashbuckling right-back who was capable of scoring goals (he scored 15 in 150 appearances for Arsenal). He also played for Brian Clough's legendary Nottingham Forest team in the late 1970s and Manchester United, where he was Sir Alex Ferguson's first signing in 1987. He eventually played for Sheffield Wednesday before taking managerial

As the decade progressed, so the number of Afro-Caribbean players increased. Paul Ince, born in Dagenham in East London in 1967, was a product of the West Ham youth academy and played at Upton Park for three seasons before a controversial move to Manchester United in 1989. The self-styled "Governor", an aggressive midfielder, was capped 53 times for England and in 1993 was

Above: Paul Ince

Far left: Viv Anderson

Left: John Fashanu

Right: Vince Hilaire

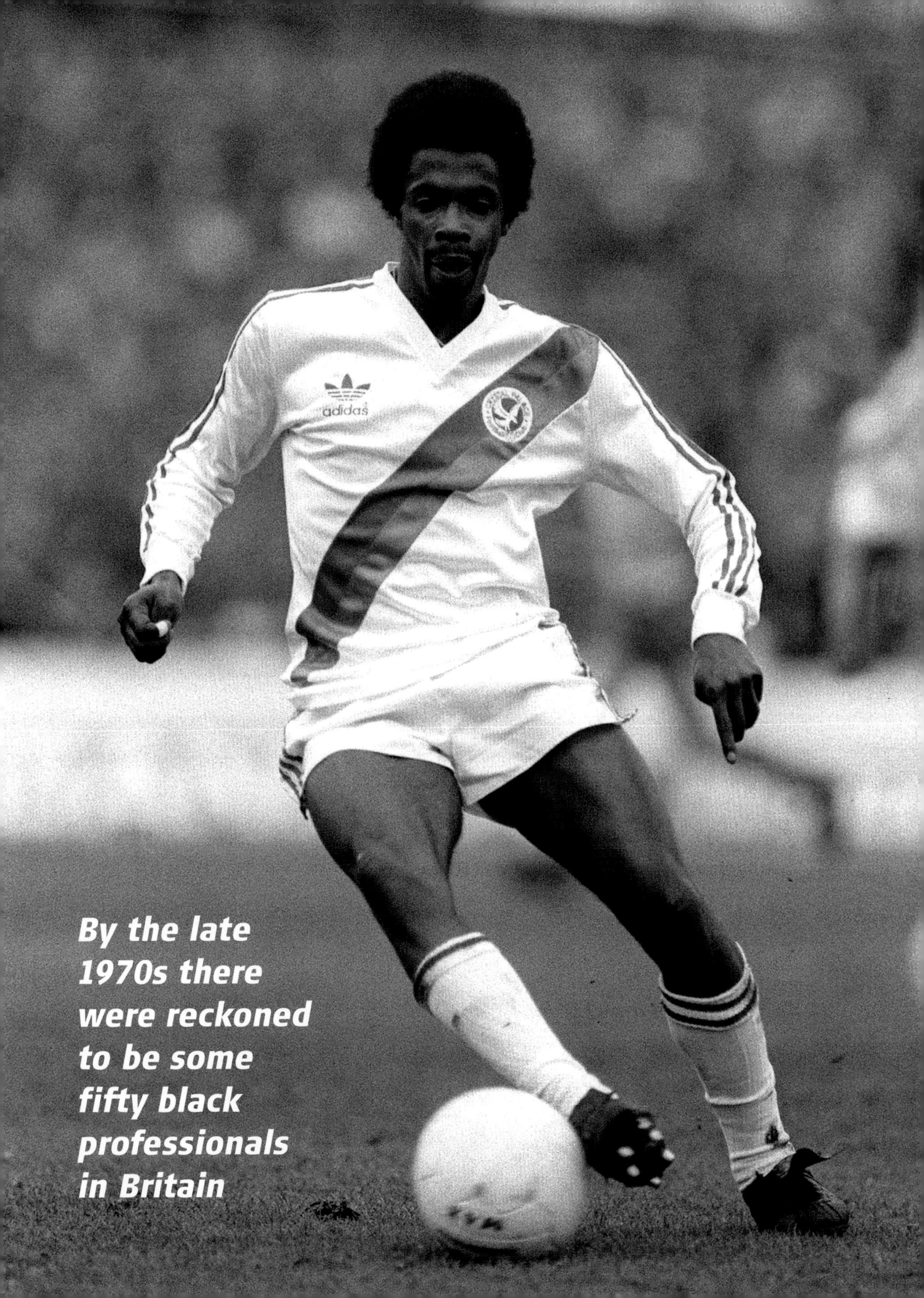

By the late 1970s there were reckoned to be some fifty black professionals in Britain

the first black player to captain the national side. He went on to play for Inter Milan, Liverpool and Wolves. Another controversial character was Justin Fashanu, who was signed by Norwich City as a precocious 14-year-old before joining Clough's Nottingham Forest in 1981 for £1 million—a record fee for a black footballer. But Fashanu and Clough did not hit it off, and a series of injuries dogged his career. He will be remembered as the first high-profile footballer to "come out" as gay at the end of the 1980s. When Clough heard of this, he famously had Fashanu escorted off the training field. Fashanu committed suicide in 1998. Justin's brother, John, was also a notable footballer, playing a pivotal role as a goal scorer in Wimbledon's celebrated "Crazy Gang" team of the late 1980s and early 1990s.

At the same time, a small number of footballers continued to come to Britain from the Caribbean to make their name. Bob Hazell arrived from Jamaica to play for Wolverhampton Wanderers and Queen's Park Rangers, where between 1979 and 1983 he became a cult hero as a tough centre-back. But of these players perhaps the most celebrated was John Barnes, born in Kingston in 1963, who came to Britain as a teenager when his father was appointed Jamaican military attaché in London. He graduated from local boys' teams via non-league football to signing as a professional with Graham Taylor's Watford in 1981. A cultured striker, Barnes played a large part in this unfashionable club's success as Watford were promoted to the First

Below left: Luther Blissett

Below right: John Barnes

Division and reached the Cup Final in 1983.

With him at Watford was another Jamaican-born forward, Luther Blissett. Unlike Barnes, Blissett spent most of his career at Watford's Vicarage Road, making 246 appearances and scoring 95 goals between 1975 and 1983. He moved to AC Milan that year for £1 million, but his time in Italy was less successful, and after a season he was sold back to Watford for £550,000. It has even been suggested that there was a mix-up between Barnes and Blissett and that the Italians thought they had signed Barnes. In total Blissett played 415 times for Watford—a club record—and scored 158 goals before going into coaching. Interestingly, his torrid time in Italy led to his name being adopted by an anarchist group.

Barnes was always a high-profile player and enjoyed the limelight

John Barnes, meanwhile, moved to Liverpool in 1987 for a fee of £900,000. By now he was an England international, having made a spectacular debut in a friendly match against Brazil in 1983. His goal, which involved outpacing several defenders and rounding the goalkeeper, made him an instant celebrity. But it also created a huge weight of expectation, which it was hard to match. In all, Barnes played 79 times for England, scoring 12 goals, but many thought that he never played his best when wearing the England shirt. For Liverpool, on the other hand, Barnes was outstanding as the team coasted to the league championship in 1987/88 with only two defeats. His pace down the left wing, together with his understanding with fellow England international Peter Beardsley, made him a key part of what was then England's undisputedly best club side.

Barnes was always a high-profile player and enjoyed the limelight. He famously rapped on Liverpool's Cup Final song *Anfield Rap* and again on *World in Motion*, New Order's No. 1 hit to celebrate England's 1990 World Cup campaign. But he also attracted a good deal of criticism from the media and England supporters, who thought that he underachieved and lacked passion when playing for his adopted country. Worse, he was the target for extremist groups and racist individuals, who repeatedly abused him. In his autobiography he recalls how he was only the second black player to appear for Liverpool and that racism was rife, even among home fans:

> *When I arrived at Anfield, racist slogans were daubed on the stadium walls: 'NF', 'White Power', 'No Wogs Allowed', 'There's No Black In the Union Jack', and 'Liverpool are White'. I expected it. Evil exists in football as in life generally. I received letters from sad old men apoplectic that blacks should represent Liverpool. 'Liverpool are all-white,' wrote one guy, echoing a general theme. 'You are crap, go back to Africa and swing from the trees.'*

Away fans were even more vitriolic, and Barnes was subjected to regular taunts, spitting and banana-throwing. He was even insulted by so-called England fans on a plane returning from an international match in South America. Much of the abuse was purely racist; some also revolved around the perception that Barnes made too little effort.

John Barnes went on to manage Celtic, without great success, and to become a TV football presenter. His autobiography, published in 1999, is a painfully honest account of the impact of racism on a uniquely talented player.

...Racist slogans were daubed on the stadium walls. I expected it. Evil exists in football as in life generally.

The Black Stereotype

Barnes' experience of prejudice was symptomatic of generally racist assumptions about black footballers stretching back, as we have seen, to Gillie Heron in the 1950s. The

Above: Stephen Bywater, Shaka Hislop, and Brian Deane lead the modern anti-racism campaign.

"received wisdom" among commentators and fans was that black players had flair and individual skills but that they were not team players, that they lacked commitment and grit. In an age when "hard" players such as Billy Bremner at Leeds or "Chopper" Harris at Chelsea were particularly revered, black footballers could easily be stereotyped as skilful but soft. According to Hunter Davies,

While I was researching "The Glory Game" in the early 1970s, I came across many football coaches who insisted black players would never make it here. They wouldn't survive the winters, so it was believed, hated muddy pitches, didn't like it up 'em, couldn't dish it out, and were generally softies, fancy dans who chickened out.

This sort of attitude is expressed in Brian

Above: Carlton Palmer

Woolnough's 1983 study of black footballers, *Black Magic*, which was supposed to be a positive tribute to the earliest players. Of Clyde Best, Woolnough observed "He is perhaps the best example of why it has taken so long for managers, coaches and the public to accept the coloured stars. Best would be brilliant one game, bad the next, and the question marks against the black players' stamina, power and determination hung over them for years."

According to Andy Hansen, "At the time [the 1970s and early 1980s] the prevailing cliché was that black players were instinctive, fast and mercurial, but lacked the 'bottle' (physical courage), commitment and cool head traditionally associated with the white English player. Black players therefore tended to feature overwhelmingly as wingers and strikers and were kept away from the more combative and responsible midfield and defensive positions." This was certainly the case with Best, Barnes, Hilaire, Cunningham and so on. Hansen adds:

One consequence of playing largely as wingers was that players such as Barnes were on the whole closer to the crowd and thus more exposed to the abusive chants, monkey noises and banana skins which elements of the crowd would throw at them.

Of course, racist fans were not the most intelligent of supporters and were often not aware of their own inconsistency in cheering their black players but abusing others. Nor were they easily persuaded that black players did have "bottle". It probably took the appearance of several players of the temperament of Paul Ince, Carlton Palmer, Ian Wright and Sol Campbell in the 1980s and 1990s to finally lay to rest the myth of the softy.

Nowadays, with players such as Patrick Vieira, Claude Makelele and Ledley King household names, it seems absurd to equate black footballers with faintheartedness or lack of commitment.

Vive la France!

When France won the World Cup in 1998 and the Euro 2000 competition commentators were surprised at the ethnic diversity within the team. There was Zinedine Zidane, born in Marseilles to Algerian immigrant parents; there was Vieira, born in Senegal, who moved to Paris at the age of eight; there was Marcel Desailly, born in Ghana. Seasoned journalist Hunter Davies wrote in 1999:

Commentators were surprised at the ethnic diversity within the team

One of the interesting things about France's World Cup winning team was the lack of Frenchmen, true Frenchmen, with blue eyes, wearing berets and a string of onions round their necks. I didn't notice many of them. What we all noticed was the large number of North Africans, such as Zidane, or black Africans, such as Desailly, or West Indians, such as Thierry Henry and Lilian Thuram. The latter two both originated from Guadeloupe, one of two French departments in the West Indies, the other being Martinique. Guadeloupe itself only has a population of 300,000, so it's done well to produce two World Cup stars.

Below: Thierry Henry and Lilian Thuram flank goalkeeper Fabien Barthez before a French international.

Henry left the Academy aged 16 and went on to a career that is now still legendary

Since then Les Bleus have counted among their squad players from Cameroon, Congo, Ivory Coast and the far-flung French Pacific colony of New Caledonia.

While the make-up of the modern French team certainly reflects the many nationalities that have made their home in France, it is also nothing new. In the 1980s Mali-born Jean Tigana was a crucial part of Bordeaux's success in the French domestic league and European Cup. He was joined there by Marius Trésor, born in 1950 in the Caribbean island of Guadeloupe. Tigana, who had previously worked as a postman and in a spaghetti factory in Marseille, won acclaim as a high-octane midfielder and was capped 52 times by France, while Trésor represented France 65 times and will be remembered for two superb goals, a headed equalizer against Brazil in 1977 and a 93rd-minute free-kick against West Germany in the semi-final, which France eventually lost on penalties.

Below: Marius Trésor

Trésor's homeland of Guadeloupe, like Martinique and mainland Guyane (French Guiana), is technically and politically part of France—as French as Normandy or Burgundy. There has always been an unrestricted flow of people between the Caribbean "overseas departments" and mainland France, and this flow has included footballers. There is also a significant community of French Caribbean people living in around Paris and other big cities, and it is from these suburbs that many of France's greatest players, past and present, have sprung.

Take Thierry Henry, for instance. His father Antoine, from Guadeloupe, and mother Marylese, Guadeloupean too but from a Martinican family, came to Paris in the early 1970s to seek work. They left the idyllic offshore island of La Désirade and ended up in the tough concrete jungle of Les Ulis, one of the many 1960s-era suburbs that surround the French capital. It was here, with his

Above: Thierry Henry

father's almost fanatical backing, that Henry, born in 1977, learned his game, playing with the other Caribbean and North African youths whose families had ended up in Les Ulis. Henry played for a local youth team, Vitry-Châtillon, where he scored a remarkable 77 goals in 26 games. From there it was a short step to be selected, as a 13-year-old, as one of the 25 boys chosen each year to go to the French Football Academy There he met Louis Saha, William Gallas and Nicolas Anelka. Gallas and Saha were also of Guadeloupean descent, while Anelka's parents were from Martinique. As a result, the four spoke French Creole together and felt a common cultural bond.

Henry left the Academy aged 16 and went on to a career that is now still legendary. Gallas made a great name for himself in Chelsea's defence, while the moody Anelka scored a profusion of goals for Paris St.-Germain, Arsenal, Real Madrid, Manchester City and Fenerbahçe in Turkey. All have played with great distinction for the French national side.

Martinique and Guadeloupe continue to produce high-quality players who make the grade both in France and further afield. Lilian Thuram was described by fellow Juventus defender as "being from another planet" (a compliment), but was in fact born in Guadeloupe in 1972. Thuram grew up in the island wanting to become a priest, then moved to France at the age of nine where his prodigious football skills took him to Monaco, Parma and Juventus, while at the same time he represented France over a hundred times. Easily one of the best defenders in the world, Thuram is also an articulate spokesman for France's disadvantaged black youth and returns frequently to Guadeloupe to be with family and friends.

Thuram cites three particular influences on his career: his mother and players Jocelyn Angloma and Bernard Lama. Angloma was born in Guadeloupe in 1965, and moved to France where he played for Lille, Paris St.-Germain, Marseille, Torino, Inter Milan and Valencia. He also played 37 times for France before retiring and taking up

Right: Lilian Thuram

Far right: Pascal Chimbonda tussles with Wayne Rooney.

Below: David Sommeil

Below right: Bernard Lama

coaching in Guadeloupe. Lama, a flamboyant goalkeeper, was born in France but spent his childhood in Guyane. After playing for a local team, he moved to Lille, where he spent eight years, and then Paris St.-Germain. He also represented France on 44 occasions. In 1997, however, Lama's career took a turn for the worse when he gave a positive result in a drugs test (he had been using cannabis) and he was suspended and lost the no. 1 spot to Fabien Barthez. Now retired, Lama has business interests in Guyane and lives there and in mainland France.

Several other French Caribbean players have enjoyed successful spells in the British game. David Sommeil of Manchester City was born in Guadeloupe, as was Wigan's Pascal Chimbonda.

France's Caribbean contingent remain firmly attached to their roots. Henry frequently returns to Guadeloupe, and more specifically La Désirade, where in 2002 a local journalist interviewed his 75-year-old grandmother, Danielle, who for thirty years worked as a cook in the local school. She spoke proudly of how Thierry funded a training school for local children and how he went swimming with old friends on the nearby beach. "Thierry hasn't got a big head," she said, "he's a star but he talks to everybody."

"Thierry hasn't got a big head," she said, "he's a star but he talks to everybody."

For Holland, the former colony of Suriname proved a rich source of footballing talent

Dutch Courage

For Holland the former colony of Suriname, which became independent in 1975, proved a rich source of footballing talent. The humid South American territory seemed to produce an endless supply of promising youngsters, most of whom had their eyes on the bright lights of Amsterdam or Rotterdam. Almost all of those who made it in Holland preferred to play for the Dutch national side, leaving Suriname with a serious deficit of top-quality players. Even so, this small nation of half a million competes creditably in CONCACAF competitions and maintains a fierce rivalry with neighbouring Guyana.

Many Surinamese left for Holland in the run-up to independence, as the Dutch opened their doors to mass migration, and about 300,000 Surinamese were thought to live in Holland by 1995. From this community emerged some of the best players ever to represent club and country in Holland, notably Ruud Gullit, Frank Rijkaard and Patrick Kluivert. All were born in Amsterdam (Kluivert was the son of a Surinamese professional footballer), and all rose through the ranks of local clubs before embarking on international careers as players and managers. Others who were born in Holland of Surinamese parentage include Mario Melchiot and Winston Bogarde.

Those who remained behind in Suriname were to come to Holland as children. Edgar Davids was born in the capital Paramaribo in 1973 but migrated to Amsterdam soon afterwards and made a name for himself first at Ajax and then AC Milan, Juventus, Barcelona, Inter Milan and Tottenham Hotspur. With his trademark goggles (worn as a precaution because of glaucoma), he became known as a highly combative, not to say aggressive, midfielder.

Other Suriname-born footballers who have made names for themselves include striker Jimmy Floyd Hasselbaink of Leeds United, Chelsea and Middlesborough fame. He was born in Paramaribo in 1972 and has one of the hardest shots in football. Like other Surinamese migrants, Hasselbaink ended up in a tough housing estate near Amsterdam when

Left: The inimitable Edgar Davids.

Right: Clarence Seedorf

Below: Barcelona coach Frank Rijkaard celebrates with his players after winning the 2005 Spanish League.

brought to Holland as a child. Hanging out with gangs and dealing in stolen goods, he was sent to a detention centre as a teenager. "My dad, who was no good, stayed in Suriname. That's why I took the wrong direction." Football saved him, he says.

There are many other instances of Surinamese talent. Defensive midfielder Clarence Seedorf (born 1976) has played for Ajax, Real Madrid and AC Milan. Defensive midfielder Aron Winter (born 1967) was capped 83 times by Holland. He played for Ajax, Lazio, Inter Milan and Ajax again before retiring in 2002. These players may have left Suriname, but their homeland remains important to them, as Seedorf revealed in a 2003 interview: "I love to go back there. It has such a calming influence, even though I only get to go back for a week in the summer. There is so much sun and greenery. And then there is my family and my grandfather who is 94-years-old."

Even the tiny islands of the Netherlands Antilles export footballers into Europe. Daniel Rijaard, for instance, plays for Den Haag in the Dutch top division.

The American Connection

"Soccer" may be baseball or basketball's poor relation in large parts of the USA, but it is on the up, particularly among women and in schools, where it is seen as less physically confrontational than American football. In fact, football has a long history in America, played by the many ethnic communities that from the outset have made up the country's population. Almost every migrant group, whether Italian, Scottish, Polish or Mexican, has a strong tradition of local football. The main problem, apart from competition from other sports, has been the logistical problem of organizing a national league and the lack of a secure fan base that might encourage

Left: Shalrie Joseph.

corporate and other investors as well as big television chains to support the sport.

Even so, professional football in the USA, strengthened in 1996 by the creation of Major League Soccer, provides another potentially lucrative avenue along which Caribbean-born players can develop their careers. In particular, the well-developed college circuit acts as a magnet to better-educated footballers in the Caribbean, who can find their college fees paid at many US universities in return for their skills on the pitch. In the past, this has caused something of a footballing brain drain in the Caribbean, as promising youngsters pack their bags and head off to college in the US. A Jamaican football website listed 36 young footballers attached to American colleges in 2003.

The structure of Major League Soccer is entirely different from that in Britain and Europe. It operates as a single entity, and players are contracted with the league rather than with the twelve individual clubs. Players are selected at "combines", where they are usually sent by colleges or other institutions and then allocated to clubs. Each MLS team is given a salary budget, and yearly salaries for players range between US$35,000 and a maximum of $280,000, with an average of $80,000. This is obviously much more than a player could expect to earn by playing in the Caribbean.

Not surprisingly, a good number of Caribbean-born players make their living in the US game. In fact, footballers have been migrating to the greener pastures of the American leagues since the 1960s, with many going from the "big two" nations of Jamaica and Trinidad & Tobago as well as a few from Haiti and elsewhere. Grenada international midfielder Shalrie Joseph, for example, plays for New England Revolution in the MLS. The US game offers invaluable openings to players

from Haiti; Jean-Philippe Peguero, Alexandre Boucicaut and Johnny Descollines have all made an impression in the American game.

In the 1970s the North American Soccer League, which eventually collapsed in 1984, offered opportunities both to big-name players from Europe at the end of their careers and to footballers from the Caribbean. Steve David, for instance, a prolific striker for Trinidad & Tobago between 1971 and 1975, played for Miami Toros, scoring an extraordinary 26 goals in 24 games, before moving to San Jose Earthquakes. The legendary Leroy Spann, who captained Trinidad & Tobago through the 1970s and 1980s, also played for San Jose Earthquakes. Nowadays, defender Avery John is with New England Revolution (he previously played in Ireland), while Cornell Glen plays for Columbus Crew.

Jamaicans also went in numbers to play in the NASL and are very much part of today's MLS scene. Reggae Boyz defender Robert Scarlett plays with Real Salt Lake, for instance, while midfielder Jermaine Hue is with Kansas City Wizards. In 2001 Colorado Rapids had three Jamaican defenders—Christopher Dawes, Robin Fraser and Steve Herdsman—on its books. Jeff Cunningham, born in Montego Bay, has even gone so far as to take out US citizenship and has represented the US national side as well as scoring regularly for Colorado Rapids. Right back Tyrone Marshall plays for Los Angeles Galaxy, having previously appeared for Colorado Rapids. Of the 1998 Reggae Boyz squad, several played in the USA, not least Walter "Blacka Pearl" Boyd, who appeared for Colorado Foxes. According to Robbie Earle and Daniel Davies, "Boyd... flew into Jamaica on the morning of a game and was usually on his way back to Denver, where he was coached by Jamaican Lorne Donaldson, later that evening. Many of his fans will tell you that Boyd paid his own way in the early days."

To the ends of the earth

Caribbean footballers are to be found all over the planet, from Scandinavia to Japan, from Russia to the Gulf States. In 2000, the Trinidad & Tobago Football Federation estimated that there were at least fifty nationals on professional contracts in Europe. Most are in Britain, but others from all over the Caribbean can end up playing football in the unlikeliest places. Wherever there is a professional league you are likely to find a footballer from Jamaica or Trinidad.

Dwight Yorke, the talisman of the Soca Warriors, earns his living in Australia, playing

Far left: Tyrone Marshall of Los Angeles Galaxy.

Left: Dwight Yorke.

Caribbean footballers are to be found all over the planet

for Sydney FC. His team mate Silvio Spann, son of Leroy, has had an exotic football career, playing briefly for Croatia's Dinamo Zagreb, then moving to Perugia and finally ending up with Yokohama FC of Japan. Brent Rahim, another Trinidad & Tobago international, has spent time at West Ham United, Scotland's Falkirk and Sofia Leviski of Bulgaria before arriving at IF Sylvia in Sweden. Jamaican Robert Scarlett was previously at Spartak Moscow. More than three decades ago, Alan "Skill" Cole, a legend in his native Jamaica, was playing for the Brazilian side Nautica. Later, the inspirational Jamaican Peter Cargill and his compatriot Paul "Tegat" Davies played professional football in Israel.

Perhaps more improbably, Trinidadian defender Atiba Charles left local team

Vibe CT105 W Connection in December for a trial with South Korean club Busan I'Park. He was following several Caribbean players, including Kelvin Jack of Trinidad and Earl Jean of St. Lucia who have had stints at Chinese clubs. Ian Lake, an international for St. Kitts & Nevis, plays for Sabah Rhinos in Malaysia, as did fellow Kittitian Keith Gumbs, who has also played in Portugal, Greece, the Netherlands and Hong Kong.

The Caribbean-British Connection

There is hardly a professional team in England, and increasingly in Scotland, that does not today boast at least one Caribbean or Caribbean-descended player. After the breakthrough decade of the 1980s increasing numbers of black players born in the UK have left their mark on the game. Of these the great majority are the sons or grandsons of migrants from the Caribbean. A player like Arsenal's Sol Campbell, one of twelve children born to Jamaican migrants, is not untypical of the current generation.

Right: Wigan's Jason Roberts celebrates an Aston Villa own goal, October 2005.

Below: Bolton's Ricardo Gardner holds back Freddie Ljungberg of Arsenal.

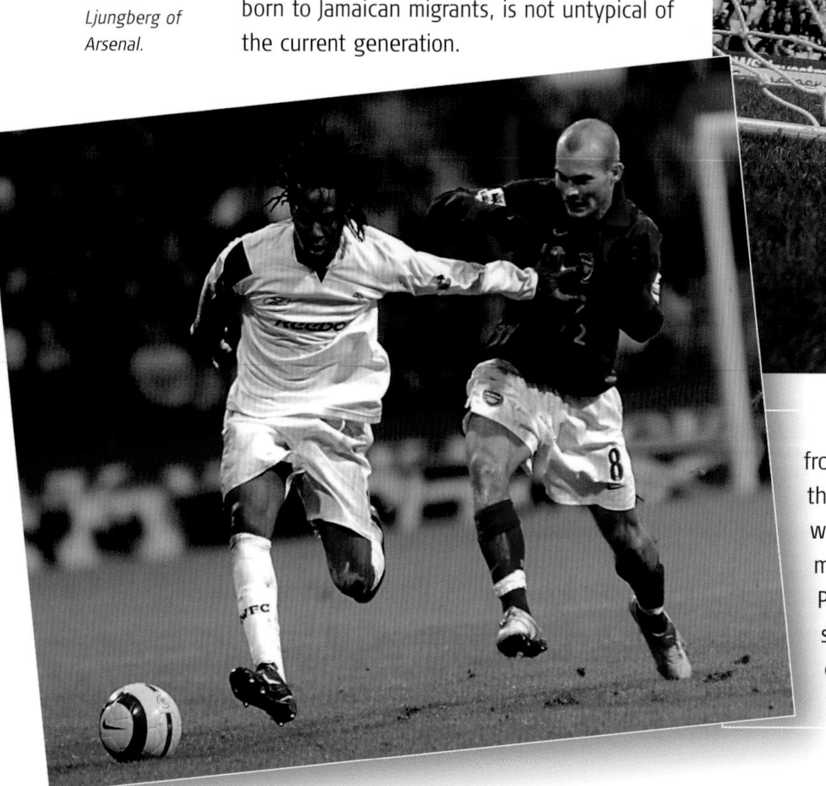

Players also continue to arrive from the Caribbean. Only those of the "highest calibre" are able to gain work permits in the UK, and this means that most are internationals. Players who have not won a significant number of international caps are sometimes refused work permits, as it is deemed that a

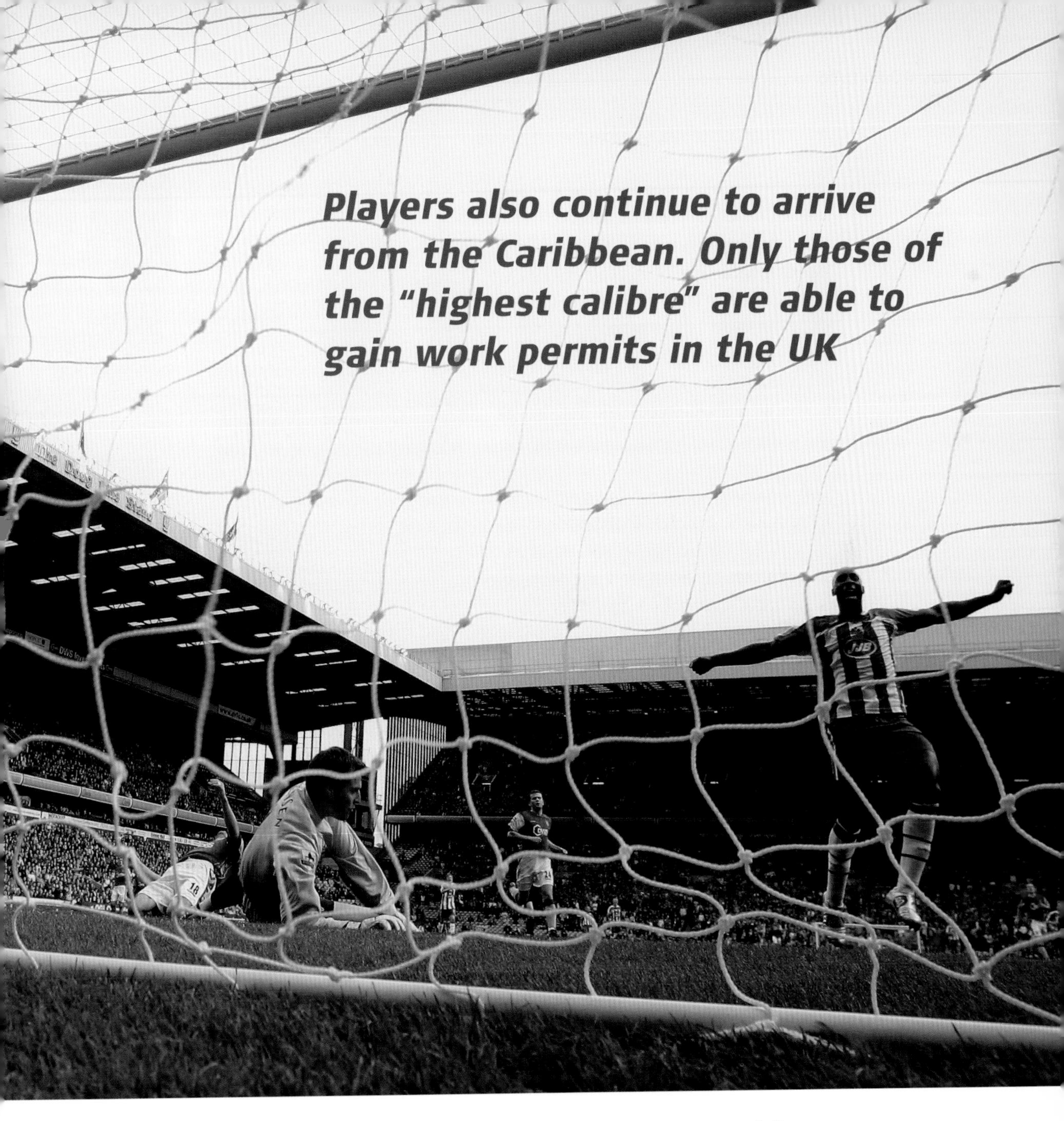

Players also continue to arrive from the Caribbean. Only those of the "highest calibre" are able to gain work permits in the UK

British national could do the same job equally well. Of the 22-man Trinidad & Tobago squad selected to face Bahrain in November 2005 thirteen were based with British sides, ranging from goalkeeper Shaka Hislop (West Ham), striker Stern John (Coventry) and Kenwyne Jones (Southampton) to veteran Russell Latapy (Falkirk), Kelvin Jack (Dundee United) and Jason Scotland (St. Johnstone).

The Jamaican national team's website (www.reaggaeboyz.com) meanwhile lists thirteen internationals employed by British clubs, of whom Ricardo Gardner (Bolton), Kevin Lisbie (Charlton) and Darren Moore (West Bromwich Albion) are perhaps the best known.

Even some of the smaller footballing territories of the Caribbean have players in the British game. There are several, we have

FILA
Dr. Martens
FILA

seen, from Guadeloupe, Martinique and Suriname. Grenada is the home of Wigan's highly rated striker Jason Roberts (Cyrille Regis' nephew), and he has played over 20 times for the national side. St. Lucia international, Ken Charlery, was a prolific scorer over several seasons in the lower divisions of the Football League. Rodney Jack of St. Vincent has appeared for Torquay, Oldham Athletic, Crewe Alexandra and various other English clubs before moving to Ireland. Following in the footsteps of Clyde Best, Shaun Goater from Bermuda won a cult following—with its own website—at Manchester City before moving to Reading and Southend.

Yet despite the large numbers of Caribbean-born and Caribbean-descended players in the British game—in 2004 it was estimated that almost 25% of players were black—there seems to be a "glass ceiling" when it comes to coaching and managerial jobs. John Barnes and Ruud Gullit aside, no black ex-player has managed a major club, and even in the lower divisions black managers are in a distinct minority. At the time of writing there were two: Keith Alexander (Lincoln) and Carlton Palmer (Mansfield). In February 2006 Leroy Rosenior, formerly of West Ham and father of Fulham's fullback Liam Rosenior, left his post at Torquay. The same situation seems to exist in coaching. Whereas several black players—Barnes, Crooks, Robbie Earle, Chris Kamara—have successfully progressed to football "punditry" on TV and radio, managerial and coaching posts seem much more restricted.

Left: Shaka Hislop

Above: Rodney Jack rides a tackle.

Left: Shaun 'the Goat' Goater

John Barnes and Ruud Gullit aside, no black ex-player has managed a major club

Return tickets

Caribbean-born footballers have been returning home to play for their national sides since the 1950s, and nowadays it is quite common for players to leave their clubs on a regular basis to represent their home country. Since the 1990s, however, this stream of returning footballers has been swelled by another current of football talent: players of Caribbean descent but born abroad.

It began with Rene Simoes' strategic decision to add professional experience and skills to the 1998 Jamaica squad by inviting players such as Robbie Earle, Deon Burton, Paul Hall and Fitzroy Simpson—all of Jamaican parentage—to join up. The Trinidadian Soca Warriors employed the same strategy, actively seeking out players in Europe and North America with a Trinidadian background who could add their abilities to those born and playing locally.

As a result, so the cynics say, players have suddenly become interested in where their grandmother was born, suspecting that it might be easier to be selected for Jamaica or Trinidad & Tobago than England. And this, they say, is particularly the case when the teams in question are likely to qualify for the World Cup finals and hence offer those players a moment of glory on the international stage rather than an obscure routine encounter with Guatemala or Anguilla.

But leaving cynicism aside, British-born players have not only contributed significantly to the success of Caribbean teams, but they have also given something back to the region and, in the process, reconnected with the culture of the parents. Robbie Earle's account of his role in the 1998 World Cup campaign with Jamaica, *One Love*, provides an illuminating insight into the pride felt by the British-born Jamaican footballers as well as the two-way culture shock experienced by them and their locally born counterparts.

One case of a returning player caught the media's eye in the 2005 Trinidad & Tobago campaign. Christopher Birchall, a striker, was born locally in Staffordshire and progressed through local sides to signing for League One side Port Vale. His grandparents had emigrated to Trinidad for work, and his mother, Jenny, was born in Port of Spain. She came to live in the UK at the age of eighteen, married a man from Liverpool and settled in the Potteries. Although Birchall was aware of his Trinidadian antecedents, it was not until a game against Wrexham, and against the giant Trinidadian defender Dennis Lawrence, that the implications of his family history became clear:

We were playing against Wrexham and one of their defenders, Dennis Lawrence, who plays for Trini, came up to me during the game. He's 6ft 7in and I thought he was going to mouth off at me. But he asked, "Have you got any Trini blood in you?" "My mum was born there," I said. "I need to speak to you after the game," he said.

The rest, as they say, is history. Lawrence duly contacted the Trinidad & Tobago authorities; Jack Warner hurried the bureaucratic side along; and Birchall was enrolled in time to score the crucial equalizer against Bahrain in the first leg of the November 2005 play-offs. "The first white man to score for Trinidad in sixty years," pointed out the British press, but when the ball screamed in, nobody was looking at Birchall's skin colour.

Could it be that British players, with no Caribbean ancestry, might soon be moving to the region to earn a living? Such was the case with Aaron Black, a former Under-19 Northern Ireland international, who signed with Trinidad's Vibe CT105 W Connection after three and a half years at Ayr United. The defender observed that "it is a very technical and fast-paced game here and the standard is extremely high." His move to Trinidad in 2005 was facilitated by Russell Latapy, but by the end of the year he was back in Northern Ireland, playing for Glenavon FC. Interestingly, Connection also had a number of Brazilians on their books, as well as players from Guyana and St. Lucia.

Above: Chris Birchall of Port Vale

Left: Leroy Rosenior

Aaron Black's Caribbean adventure may have been short-lived, but as Caribbean professional football grows in strength, it is by no means impossible that the flow of footballing talent may at last be reversed.

The first white man to score for Trinidad in sixty years...

Part Four

Across The Region: A Football Guide

The FIFA World Ranking includes all the world's FIFA-affiliated national sides and is updated periodically to take account of recent results. In December 2005, the ranking numbered 205 teams from Brazil (1) to American Samoa (205). Trinidad & Tobago had risen two places (51), while Jamaica had fallen three (43). Guadeloupe, Martinique and French Guiana are not included, as they come under the aegis of the French national side (5th).

Below: Clifton Sandvliet scores for Suriname against Aruba, Paramaribo, March 2004.

Caribbean National Sides

Anguilla

FIFA world ranking: *197*

With a population of just over 12,000, tiny Anguilla does not have a large number of footballers. An amateur league exists, with teams colourfully called Roaring Lions and Attackers, but the island's international profile is distinctly low. Hopes in the 2006 World Cup were dashed by a 6-0 defeat at the hands of the Dominican Republic. The national side would rather forget a 1998 0-14 result against Guyana. News that a new $1.5-million stadium and training facility, funded by FIFA's Goal programme, is under way will no doubt encourage players and fans alike.

Antigua & Barbuda

FIFA world ranking: *155*

The twin-island state has been rather unpredictable in international performances, managing to beat Haiti in 1984 but suffering an 8-1 aggregate thrashing at the hands of Guatemala in 2000. The team has taken part in every World Cup qualifying contest since 1974 but has come away with little success. This is perhaps hardly surprising, given the repeated allegations of incompetence and corruption levelled against the country's football association by local journalists. Meanwhile, a local amateur league organizes various divisions and an FA Cup, with teams such as West Ham and Villa Lions reflecting a strong British influence.

Left: Women's football in Bermuda.

Above: Never too young to tackle in Bermuda.

Aruba

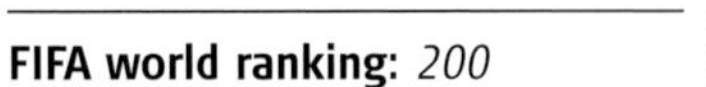

FIFA world ranking: *200*

Football has a long history in this former Dutch colony, with the first international, against Suriname dating back to 1934. The first game is thought to have taken place in 1908. But the sport has always had to compete with baseball for popular support, and the national side has largely failed to lift the island out of the FIFA ranking doldrums. Their particular nemesis is the larger and more powerful Suriname, who beat them by an aggregate 10-2 in the CONCACAF qualifying round for Germany 2006.

Bahamas

FIFA world ranking: *192*

One of several Caribbean teams propping up the FIFA ranking table, the Bahamas have yet to prove themselves at international level. They managed to beat the Turks & Caicos Islands 3-0 in 1999, but when meeting stiffer opposition have tended to capitulate. In the qualifiers for the 2002 World Cup the Bahamas did overcome the minnows of Anguilla, but then lost 9-0 and 4-0 to Haiti. Their record defeat in a single game was at the hands of Mexico, who finished 13-0 ahead. Despite poor international form, football is well entrenched over the many islands that make up the nation, with several leagues and a well-organized women's league run by the Bahamas Football Association with considerable support from FIFA's Goal.

Barbados

FIFA world ranking: *119*

Football is well run by the long-established Barbados Football Association, and local amateur teams such as Paradise and Notre Dame SC compete keenly. The national side has enjoyed some memorable moments as it has tried to qualify for the World Cup since 1978. In the run-up to the 1998 France finals Barbados' "Bajan Braves" were knocked out by Jamaica, who eventually went through. Four years later, things went better for Barbados as the team knocked out Grenada, Aruba and Cuba. Even better, in the next round they beat Costa Rica before running out of steam. A short-lived 2006 campaign saw Barbados bow out to St. Kitts & Nevis, but Barbados is tipped as a team for the future.

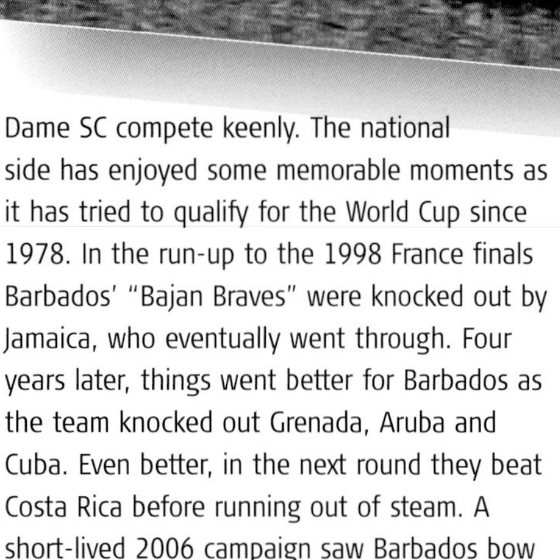

Their record defeat in a single game was at the hands of Mexico, who finished 13-0 ahead

Bermuda

FIFA world ranking: *158*

The homeland of the legendary Clyde Best, Bermuda has a long and honourable football history, stretching back to the founding of its football association in 1928. The island's best attempt at qualifying for the World Cup finals came in 1994, when they beat Haiti and Antigua & Barbuda before going into the next round where they drew with Jamaica and even beat the team that eventually went through: El Salvador. Domestically there are four leagues, mostly amateur and parish-based, with active women's and youth competitions.

British Virgin Islands

FIFA world ranking: *163*

The small population of the British-administered territory makes a strong international presence unlikely, but even so, the BVI have enjoyed their moments of triumph, notably a 5-0 victory over Puerto Rico in 1999. Bermuda, however, has always been a thorn in their flesh, beating them 5-1 and 9-0 in the 2002 qualifiers. The game is well developed on a local level, with leagues on the two main islands, Tortola and Virgin Gorda, and a strong administrative structure in place for developing women's and youth football.

Cayman Islands

FIFA world ranking: *176*

The Caymans have had the misfortune to be geographically close to Cuba and have been drawn against the Cubans with predictable regularity. In both the 1998 and 2002 qualifying rounds they fell at the first hurdle to their much bigger Spanish-speaking neighbours. The organized sport is not very old at international level in the Cayman Islands (the local football association only joined FIFA in 1992), but there is a vibrant local scene, with the intellectual-sounding Scholars International one of the leading sides.

Cuba

FIFA world ranking: *75*

Cubans are good at all sports, as anyone who follows athletics, boxing or baseball will testify, and although football is far from being the island's no.1 game, Cuba is capable of producing a strong team. It was, of course, the first Caribbean country to send a team to the World Cup finals, back in 1938, but since then it has not been able to repeat the experience, and although spirited campaigns were mounted in the 1998, 2002 and 2006 qualifiers, the Cubans came away each time empty-handed. Football is played on an entirely amateur basis, with each of the island's provinces putting a team forward for the national championship. The current name to watch out for is striker Lester Moré. Interestingly, a Cuban player, Erich Hernández, holds the current world record for football head juggling, making 146 consecutive touches in 30 seconds in 2005.

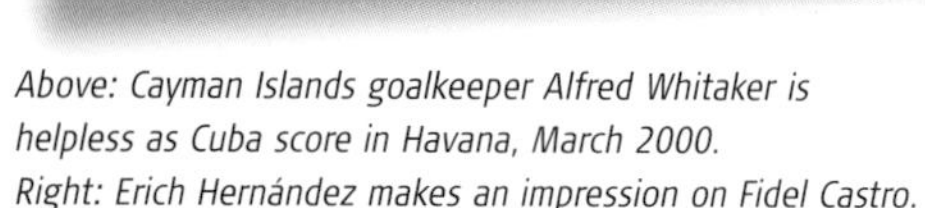

Above: Cayman Islands goalkeeper Alfred Whitaker is helpless as Cuba score in Havana, March 2000.
Right: Erich Hernández makes an impression on Fidel Castro.

Cuba was the first Caribbean country to send a team to the World Cup finals, back in 1938

Above: The national sides of Dominica (left) and Guyana prior to a friendly, which Guyana won 3-0.

Dominica

FIFA world ranking: *169*

The lush, volcanic island of Dominica might seem too mountainous to have many football pitches, but the national team has performed creditably since 1998, when it started its World Cup qualifying campaigns. That year they beat Antigua & Barbuda before losing to Barbados. In 2000 they faced Haiti and lost 4-0 over two legs. The team can look back with pride to 1997 when Dominica dispatched the British Virgin Islands 6-1, but will remember their 2006 qualifying bid with less pleasure: they lost 10-0 and 8-0 to Mexico in what most commentators saw as the classic David versus Goliath contest.

They lost 10-0 and 8-0 to Mexico in what most saw as the classic David versus Goliath contest

Dominican Republic

FIFA world ranking: *173*

Football comes about fifth in the Dominican Republic's list of favourite sports behind baseball, basketball, volleyball and athletics. Some local amateur teams do play, but there is little evidence of a real football culture, probably because the country looks towards the USA for many of its influences. Dominican aspirations in World Cup qualifiers have been quickly frustrated, with defeat at the hands of Puerto Rico in the 1994 contest and Trinidad & Tobago in 1998 and 2002. The size of the country, together with recent investment by FIFA, suggests that the Dominican Republic should be a force to be reckoned with—if only its inhabitants liked football.

Grenada

FIFA world ranking: *150*

The "Spice Boyz" have not yet been able to emulate the success of their Jamaican counterparts, but for a very small island, Grenada has achieved some very creditable results, beating Guyana on several occasions and even giving the USA a hard-fought contest in the 2006 qualifiers. Jason Roberts, of Wigan Athletic fame, is the island's best-known footballing export, but there are several others who play in Europe and the USA. League and cup football is well-established, featuring Queen's Park Rangers and Ball Dogs among others.

Guadeloupe

FIFA world ranking: *N/A*

The French overseas département of Guadeloupe has been turning out world-class players for many decades, some born there, others the sons of Guadeloupean emigrants in France. As part of France, Guadeloupe has not affiliated to FIFA but plays in CONCACAF competitions and local friendlies, often with considerable success. The territory's league contains 14 teams, and the best of these, such as AS Gosier, compete with sides from fellow overseas department Martinique. Teams are also eligible to enter the Coupe de France, but none has yet made it into the last 32. The relative prosperity of Guadeloupe, due in large part to extensive subsidies from mainland France, allows above-average development in terms of youth training and infrastructure.

Guyana

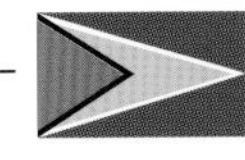

FIFA world ranking: *167*

Cricket overshadows football here, despite the country's proximity to footballing giant, Brazil.

Above: Happy trophy winners, Guyana.

Although the Guyanese (then colonial British Guiana) were among the first to form a football association, the country has had a marked lack of success in international competitions, losing all qualifying World Cup games since 1980. To make matters worse, neighbouring Suriname beat them in the 1982, 1986 and 1990 competitions. Tempers flared in 2004 when Grenada went to play in Guyana, only for there to be inadequate food provided for their players. According to the *Guyana Chronicle*, Grenada's manager had to go and buy bread and cheese for his team on the morning of the match. Even so, the local Guyana Football Federation is busy supporting coaching and women's football.

Since the heroics of 1974, Haitian teams have had trouble getting out of the CONCACAF qualifiers

Guyane (French Guiana)

FIFA world ranking: *N/A*

Perhaps best known for its notorious penal colony and the exploits of "Papillon", France's South American enclave is not part of FIFA but is nonetheless very much part of the Caribbean football scene, entering teams for the CONCACAF Gold Cup competition and playing friendless across the region. There is a strong domestic league, and the territory's leading teams take on clubs from Guadeloupe and Martinique. Over the years French Guiana has contributed several outstanding players to the French national side, not least flamboyant goalkeeper Bernard Lama.

Haiti

FIFA world ranking: *91*

Haitian football had been badly hit by decades of political instability and permanent poverty, which prevent investment in the game. Even so, a 16-team league usually manages to compete, with Racing Club and Violette the best-known sides. One recent bright spot was when Brazil—ever Haitian's second favourite team—came to play a "peace match" with the national side, which the Brazilians won 6-0. Haitian players continue to do well in US professional football and, occasionally, in Europe. Since the heroics of 1974, however, Haitian teams have had trouble getting out of the CONCACAF preliminary qualifying rounds, most recently being beaten by Jamaica.

Above: Haitian youths play football by a mural of Jean-Bertrand Aristide.

Jamaica

FIFA world ranking: *43*

Undoubtedly one of the Caribbean's "big two", Jamaica was the first English-speaking team to go all the way to the World Cup

Above: A contest in the Wray & Nephew Premier League.

finals in 1998. Since then the Reggae Boyz have struggled to find the consistency and goal-scoring power to get them back into the top flight. The 2006 qualifying campaign was a major disappointment, with below-par performances against the USA and Panama blighting any chance of qualifying. Critics blame the game's administrators, lack of investment and a poor balance of foreign-based and local talent for Jamaica's recent woes, but it would be very unwise to assume that the island will not bounce back from adversity. The semi-professional Wray & Nephew Premier League is a breeding ground for talent, and a host of Jamaicans play professional football around the world.

Martinique

FIFA world ranking: *N/A*

The mirror image of Guadeloupe, Martinique is home to a well-established league, the best teams competing with their Guadeloupean counterparts. Martinique has produced slightly fewer world-class players than Guadeloupe, but even so individuals like David Régis and Matthieu Louis-Jean have played successfully overseas. The island is not FIFA-affiliated but presents strong opposition in CONCACAF Gold Cup competitions and local friendlies. The Dillon stadium in Fort-de-France, where France beat Costa Rica 3-2 in a November 2005 friendly match, is one of the Caribbean's best.

Montserrat

FIFA world ranking: *202*

Volcano-devastated Montserrat (population approx. 10,000) is almost always at the bottom of the FIFA ranking. Indeed, it seems almost proud of this distinction and in 2002 organized a match, dubbed "The Other Final", with fellow strugglers Bhutan. Bhutan won 4-0. With its only football pitch rendered unplayable by the volcano and most of the capital abandoned, it is hardly surprising that the Montserratians have made little headway. Their 2006 campaign ended with a 6-1 defeat to the Dominican Republic (their home game was played in Trinidad).

Netherlands Antilles

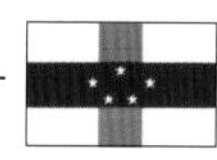

FIFA world ranking: *166*

The Dutch-affiliated islands of Curaçao, Bonaire, Sint Eustatius, Saba and Sint Maarten are scattered across the Caribbean, but despite their small size they have produced a good many excellent players. The heyday was the 1940s and 1950s, when Curaçao won the Pan-American Games, with the legendary Ergilio Hato, a.k.a "the black panther", in goal. The Netherlands Antilles are still capable of springing the occasional surprise, but have struggled in recent contests, failing to progress beyond the CONCACAF first round. FIFA-funded development plans by the Antillian FA may bring a return of the glory days.

Puerto Rico

FIFA world ranking: *193*

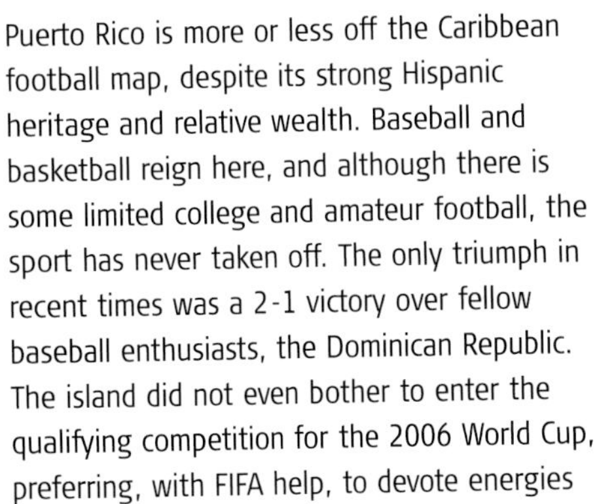

Puerto Rico is more or less off the Caribbean football map, despite its strong Hispanic heritage and relative wealth. Baseball and basketball reign here, and although there is some limited college and amateur football, the sport has never taken off. The only triumph in recent times was a 2-1 victory over fellow baseball enthusiasts, the Dominican Republic. The island did not even bother to enter the qualifying competition for the 2006 World Cup, preferring, with FIFA help, to devote energies to building up the sport at local level.

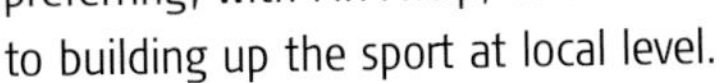

St. Kitts & Nevis

FIFA world ranking: *128*

The twin-island state had been improving steadily prior to the 2006 campaign, with wins over Trinidad & Tobago and Haiti, but a tough semi-final group of Mexico, Trinidad & Tobago and St. Vincent saw the Kittitians beaten in all games despite the presence of a handful of professionals who earn their living overseas. On the whole, though, football has been on the up since St. Kitts & Nevis affiliated to FIFA in 1998, and there are 29 teams in the football association's four divisions, including the distinctively named Rastafari Structure FC.

Football has been on the up since St. Kitts & Nevis affiliated to FIFA

St. Lucia

FIFA world ranking: *125*

Relative newcomers to organized international football, St. Lucia only joined FIFA in 1988. Since then the island's national team has enjoyed occasional success, mostly against

Below: Serious training in St. Kitts.

neighbours in the Eastern Caribbean, but also, more notably, against Suriname in 2001, whom they beat 1-0. They also managed to rout the US Virgin Islands that year, notching up a 14-1 result. Under the aegis of an energetic football association, St. Lucia is considered one of the best of the smaller-island teams.

St. Vincent & The Grenadines

FIFA world ranking: *126*

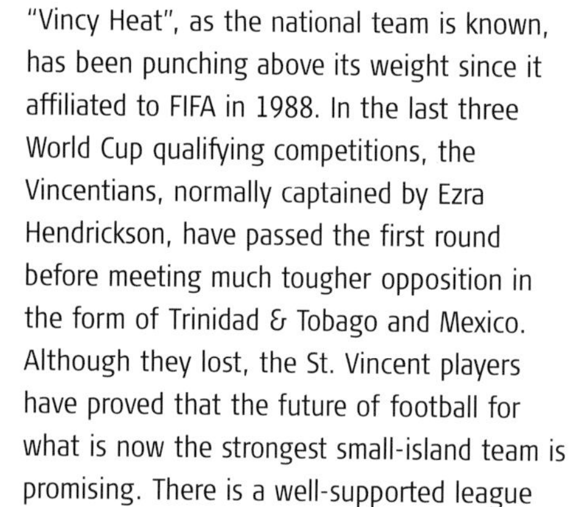

"Vincy Heat", as the national team is known, has been punching above its weight since it affiliated to FIFA in 1988. In the last three World Cup qualifying competitions, the Vincentians, normally captained by Ezra Hendrickson, have passed the first round before meeting much tougher opposition in the form of Trinidad & Tobago and Mexico. Although they lost, the St. Vincent players have proved that the future of football for what is now the strongest small-island team is promising. There is a well-supported league system across St. Vincent and the smaller Grenadine islands, with youth and women's football prominent.

Suriname

FIFA world ranking: *151*

Since the 1970s this former Dutch colony has been a conveyor belt of footballing talent, producing several world-class players. The problem, however, is that almost all of them have left to play both in and for Holland. The sporting brain drain has left Suriname on the periphery of world football, confined for the most part to competing against–and beating–neighbouring Guyana. There is, however, a well organized domestic league, with the most successful club being SV Robinhood, based in the capital Paramaribo.

Above: Northern United All Stars of Gros Islet, St. Lucia, 2005 CONCACAF Club Champions semi-finalists.

Above left: Ezra Hendrickson of St. Vincent (right).

Left: Action from the Turks and Caicos Islands.

Trinidad & Tobago

FIFA world ranking: *51*

Since the 1970s Trinidad & Tobago has fought with Jamaica for the Caribbean no. 1 spot, and if the Reggae Boyz came out top in 1998, 2006 is the year of the Soca Warriors. A change of coach, an influx of foreign-based players and a late surge saw them squeeze into the Germany 2006 finals via a two-leg play-off with Bahrain. Football in the twin-island state is more developed than anywhere else, with a small professional league and a plethora of local, amateur and semi-professional divisions. Trinidadian footballers earn their living around the world, but particularly in England and Scotland. It remains to be seen whether the country can build on the success of 2006, but it is to be hoped that the money and goodwill generated by the 2006 World Cup will lead to the construction of solid foundations for the future.

Turks & Caicos Islands

FIFA world ranking: *203*

Ranked even lower than fellow British overseas territory Montserrat, the Turks & Caicos, with about 20,000 inhabitants, are not big regional players. Their bid to qualify for the 2002 World Cup ended abruptly with a two-leg 14-0 thrashing at the hands of St. Kitts & Nevis. The 2006 campaign was rather better, as a battling two-match encounter with Haiti ended in a more respectable 0-7 score line. Recent FIFA funding for the development of facilities and coaching will encourage football devotees in one of the world's smaller sporting outposts. Men's, women's and youth football is already well-organized by an energetic football association.

US Virgin Islands

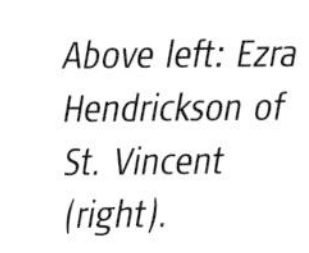

FIFA world ranking: *195*

One of the world's least successful teams, the USVI are hampered by a small population and a lack of football culture, having only affiliated to FIFA in 1998. Since then they have managed to beat their natural rivals, the British Virgin Islands, but have been soundly thrashed elsewhere, by St. Vincent & the Grenadines and St. Kitts & Nevis. The islands' football association reportedly had trouble fielding a side in 2003 against the BVI, and a proposed four-island contest was called off. Things can only get better.

Further Reading

Arthur, Charles. "The Man who Beat Dino Zoff", in *Libète: A Haiti Anthology*. London: LAB, 1999.

Barnes, John. *John Barnes: The Autobiography*. London: Headline, 1999.

Brown, Paul. *Balls: Tales from Football's Nether Regions*. Edinburgh, Mainstream, 2004.

Davies, Hunter. *Boots, Balls & Haircuts: An Illustrated History of Football from Here to Now*. London: Cassell, 2003.

Derbyshire, Oliver. *Thierry Henry*. London: Blake, 2005.

Earle, Robbie and **Daniel Davies**. *One Love: The Reggae Boyz, An Incredible Soccer Journey*. London: Andre Deutsch, 1998.

Galeano, Eduardo. *Football in Sun and Shadow: An Emotional History of World Cup Football*. London: Fourth Estate, 1998.

Glanville, Brian. *The Sunday Times History of the World Cup*. London, Times Newspapers Ltd, 1973.

Vasili, Phil. *Colouring over the White Line: The History of Black Footballers in Britain*. Edinburgh: Mainstream, 2000.

Woolnough, Brian. *Black Magic: England's Black Footballers*. London: Pelham Books, 1983.

Useful Websites

www.fifaworldcup.yahoo.com
The official World Cup site

www.futsalplanet.com
Site dedicated to the five-a-side game

www.reggaeboyz.com
For all news and views on Jamaican football

www.tnt.fifa.com
Site of the Trinidad & Tobago Football Federation

Photography

The authors and publishers would like to thank the following for permission to reproduce photographs their photographic material:

Action Images pp. 2, 50/51, 64(l)
Action Plus pp. Title page (rm), contents page, 23, 26/27, 26(b), 28, (t), 29, 31, 32/33,48, 62(t), 64/65, 70/71, 73(b), 75(t), 82
Alamy pp. 14 (tl, bl), Chapter 2 & 3 title page, 54, 87
Camera Press pp. 55, 66/67,
Corbis pp. Title page (lm, r), end of preface, 8 (t), 5(r), 10/ 11, 28(b), 35, 36, 68, 75(t, b), 78/79, 90(b), 94/95, 99(l),
Bryan Cumming pp. 45 (t, b), 96
Everald 'Gally' Cummings pp. 38 (inset), 41(b),
Empics pp. 5 (l), 6/7, 7(r), 8(b), 14/15, 16, 20/21, 21(b), 20(t), 44, 57(t, b), 69, 72(b), 73(t), 76/77,
Shaun Fuentes pp. 1 (t), 42 /43, 43(r)
James Ferguson p. 85
Getty Images pp. 1 (b), 2, 3, 4(tl, tr, b), 9, 12, 22/23, 58(l), 59, 60/61, 70, 87, 80/81, 80(b),
Guyana Football Federation pp. 92, 93
Jamaica Gleaner pp. 38/39, 40, 41(t), 53
Shaka Hislop p. Introduction
IstockPhoto.com pp. Title Pages (1 and 2), imprint page
Sterling Swan pp. Chapter 4 title page, pp88-9
Offside pp. 18/19, 18(b), 26, 27, 62(bl, br), 63, 84
Tinnie Percival pp. **35**, 47, 49, 97
Professional Sport Library pp. 83 (b)
Rex pp. 72 (t), 74,
David Sabir pp. 58(r)
Scottish Football Museum pp. Half Title page, 56
St Lucia F.A. p. 99(r)
T.C.I.F.A pp. 52, 98
TopFoto pp. Title page (insert l), 24, 25, 82/83,
Cover: **Alamy, Corbis, Istock, Scottish Football Museum, Sterling Swan**